I0003234

DEEP LEARNING

WITH PYTHON

*Comprehensive Beginners Guide
to Learn and Understand the
Realms of Deep Learning with Python*

Brian Walker

Table of Contents

Introduction

There are about one thousand and one scenarios on how the world might end.

Some say the world will end by fire, with a meteor hitting the planet out of nowhere.

Others believe mankind's biggest threat is mankind itself.

And then there are also those who believe we will be outlived by our most precious, ambitious, and Godlike project ever: artificial intelligence.

Beyond Terminator and Skynet, beyond TV shows depicting robots taking over the world, beyond Asimov and beyond all fictional works on the topic, one thing is for absolute certainty, artificial intelligence is here, it is much more present in your life than you may think it is. Chances are, it is here to stay as well.

AI should not be perceived as a malevolent "existence," in any way, though. Rather than that, AI should be seen as an existence that simply helps mankind move forward.

We might never be able to find the solution to traveling beyond the speed of light to discover if we're the only ones in the Universe - but a very smart AI might.

We might never be able to find a universal cure to cancer - but a very smart AI might.

We might never be able to learn who we truly come from - but a very smart AI might.

Take every question mankind has ever had - a very well programmed AI might actually be able to answer it.

Unlike human intelligence, AI intelligence is on self-growth mode. The more it learns, the smarter it becomes, and it's an endless, nearly infinite cycle of information that is being filtered and filtered through the networks of an AI that makes it more powerful.

Sure, everything is finite, and artificial intelligence is no exception. But even so, even with the computational limits of 2019, an AI might be better at predicting a series of outcomes than any other human.

Artificial intelligence takes many shapes and forms. At this point in its evolution, machine learning and deep learning are two of the most common shapes it takes. This is primarily because we are at a point where we have discovered how to create networks of information that can actually be filtered and processed just as a normal *human* cognitive process would be.

Beyond all those shapes and forms of AI, though, this entire concept is built based on a few basic ideas:

- Information is power

- Neural networks can imitate the human brain

- Programmers can create machine programs that enable them to filter information in a specific way, that allows them to draw conclusions and grow their learning based on that

Hopefully, the book at hand will help you gain a better understanding of the grand scheme of deep learning - and even more specifically, how deep learning connects to Python, one of the single most popular programming languages of the moment.

I have structured the book in a way that allows you to make sense of everything in the most logical way possible.

The first chapter is all about explaining Python, a programming language that continues to grow in popularity with every year that passes. We will explain why Python is a high-level language, what a program is, how debugging works, and how programming languages and actual "human" languages are much more similar (and definitely different), than they might seem.

Further on, we will move into why Python is a good solution for a wide range of applications and why so many programmers, advanced or not, turn to this language when it comes with a very generous array of options.

3

While this book does not necessarily aim to be a Python manual, I will dedicate a chapter to teaching you the absolute basics of Python programming, starting with programming and what it is, and isn't, and ending with the very first steps you should make to create a Python program.

Next, we will dive a little deeper into how Python elements are organized. This chapter is very important because it will show you some of the main characteristics that connect Python to the world of deep learning. Which, as you will see, can get along very well with this very specific programming language.

The second half of the book changes the focus from Python to artificial intelligence. First, we will explain what artificial intelligence is and how its current landscape looks like. Then, we will move a little deeper into machine learning as a branch of AI, and, once that is done, we will move a little deeper into in-depth learning as a branch of machine learning itself.

Eventually, we will begin to close the circle back to Python and explain some of the basic concepts behind deep learning programming, as well as how deep learning programming happens in Python in particular.

Because this book's main purpose is that of helping you understand deep learning not just from the point of view of a programmer, but through the "filter," of programming in general, I will also dedicate one last chapter to a topic I consider to be very important to the understanding of artificial intelligence in general: AI ethics.

Like it or not, artificial intelligence is happening unequivocally. It's here to stay, it's here to change your life as much as it will change the life of your parents and that of your children.

The world is slowly moving towards a fully automated mechanism in all respects. Soon enough, our children will be educated by artificial intelligence, and our hospitals will be so automatic you will barely see a doctor. There might be decades, and maybe even more than that, before we reach a point where the human touch is entirely removed from most day to day actions, but that the future is as plausible as rain on an October day.

The ethical issues I want to approach in the end of this book are there to help you understand that AI will definitely affect some areas of your life, or of the life of someone you love. DO keep in mind, however, that I do not intend to scare you off, or prevent you from becoming the best deep learning programmer in the world: that chapter's purpose is of helping you become the best *and* the most ethical programmer in the world.

As a programmer, you are working in a field that is so exciting, you shape the very future of mankind. It sounds grander than life and slightly dramatic, but that doesn't make it any less true. And, as a pioneer of the final tech frontier, you should be among those who raise their voices and point out the need for AI ethics *now*, before it's too late.

Finally, before we dive into the actual book, I want to say that you should expect the road ahead of you to be a little bumpy. Python is, without a doubt, one of the easiest programming languages to learn, precisely because it is intuitive and clear. However, if you want to become an actual expert at this, you will have to go beyond the basics presented in this book.

Like with every new topic in your life, Python will have a learning curve - but, the more you learn and practice, the better it will become...and obviously, the better *you* will become. Python, deep learning, and this entire world of artificial intelligence might be new to you - but that's not a good reason to be lazy about it.

Practice, practice, practice! Read, read, read, and then go back to practice!

Same as a machine learning to think like a human, you will have to be a human who learns how to think like a machine. So yes, it makes perfect sense that programming might not come as second nature to you. But it also makes perfect sense that you stay curious about it, especially since it's truly one of the best jobs to work in.

- It has clear future perspective

- It has a lot of room on the market

- It provides you with plenty of room to grow

- It is quite fascinating, especially in the context of deep learning

I genuinely hope this book will make you thirsty for knowledge and for practice. While I did not want to delve into the technicalities of Python and deep learning, I sure hope that everything presented in this book will lay a solid foundation for you as a future novice in the world of Python deep learning programming.

Don't expect this to be the easiest thing you have ever done. Don't expect to wake up one day and be able to program intricate neural networks into smart apps that help save lives. Don't expect to speak Python in 21 days like spam emails promise you to speak Italian and Spanish.

But *do* expect Python to change your life for the better. To help you find a job that is actually exciting in a field that is downright amazing. To help you live a better life financially. To help you work with amazingly smart people. To help you open the gates to the future and feel like you are part of something *bigger, better, brighter.*

Expect this book to shift your perspectives on how modern programming works and why it is perfect the way it is. Expect this book to help you *win.*

Expect this book to be the beginning of your future.

Chapter 1

What is Python and How Is It Used?

Python is a high-level and general purpose language used in programming. Although nearly three decades old at this point, Python is one of the more recent programming languages, and it is used in very modern applications. As you will see later on in this book, Python is one of the primary languages used in machine learning and deep learning.

The main philosophy behind Python emphasizes its code readability, mostly enabled by the significant whitespace concept that is frequently used when programming with this specific language. To help programmers write logical code that is clear and straightforward, Python is a language construct that uses an object-oriented approach.

Aside from its basics, Python is also considered to be:

- Dynamically typed (meaning that it executes some programming behaviors at runtime, as opposed to static typed programming languages that execute the same behaviors during the compilation).

- Garbage-collected (meaning that it functions as an automatic memory management system, where the collector reclaims objects that are not being used by the program anymore).

Python is also a programming language that supports more than one programming paradigms - such as procedural, functional, or object-oriented.

Because it comes with a very large standard library, Python is very frequently referred to as, "batteries included." In fact, it is this precise impressive standard library that makes Python a preference in a multitude of applications.

The first version of Python was released at the end of the 1980s and it was created by Guido van Rossum in Netherlands. Considered to be a successor of the, "ancient" ABC language, Python was also upgraded in 2000, when it introduced new features - such as list comprehensions or the possibility of collecting reference cycles using a garbage collection system.

In 2008, Python was upgraded once again, but its new version is not fully backward compatible. In other words, codes that were written on Python 2 do not run well on Python 3 - and for this reason, Python 2 will continue to have support until 2020.

Python was led by its inventor, Van Rossum, until 2018, when he announced his permanent vacation from being the sole lead developer in the company. At the moment, Python is led by a so-called, "Steering Council," headed up by five men: Brett Cannon, Barry Warsaw, Nick Coghlan, Carol Willing, and Van Rossum himself.

Aside from the ultra-large library Python comes with, its multi-paradigm nature makes it a common choice in the development of a lot of applications - some of which are very complex.

At its core, however, Python is relatively easy to learn, especially if you have at least some basic programming knowledge at this point. As you will see throughout this book, things might get confusing at some point - but I strongly encourage you to stick to learning and keep on practicing. The more exercises you make in the art of coding with Python, the better and more complex your code will become.

Python's main concepts are based on the, "Zen of Python," a document that includes a series of aphorisms, including the following:

- Simple is better than complex

- Beautiful is better than ugly

- Readability counts

- Complex is better than complicated[1]

...and so on.

Clearly, Python focuses a lot on keeping things clear and clean in terms of how the code is structured and how it looks once it is laid down. Obviously, this is not about aesthetics, but about the willingness to create a programming language that makes it easier for any Python developer to work with a code when they pick it up and see it for the first time.

Python is also quite modular and extensible because not all of its functionalities are built into its core. This makes this programming

---

[1] PEP 20 -- The Zen of Python. (2019). Retrieved from https://www.python.org/dev/peps/pep-0020/

language common among those who want to add programming interfaces to applications that already exist.

The entire design philosophy of Python is based on the concept that the syntax and grammar should be as de-cluttered whenever possible. According to the Python, there should be only one obvious way to write code, as opposed to other programming languages, which admit that there is more than one way to write code. In the Python culture, something that is, "clever," is not necessarily synonymous with, "good."

In the end, Python comes down to one very important feature: it should be fun to use. Even its name is drawn from a comedic group (Monty Python), which is sometimes referenced in tutorials as well (e.g. examples that talk about spam and eggs instead of "foo and bar," which is also related to a Monty Python sketch).

Sometimes, the Python community uses the term, "pythonic" - and this means that the code is natural, it has fluency, it is readable, and that it uses Python idioms correctly, conforming to the minimalist philosophy behind Python. If something is, "unpythonic," on the other hand, it means that the code is hard to read or has a rough transcription.

To continue the series of fun pun examples from the world of Python, I will also add here that users who admire Python and use it at an experienced level are sometimes called, "Pythonists," "Pythoneers," or "Pythonistas."

Hopefully, this book will help you take a first step toward becoming one of the proud bearers of one of the aforementioned Grand Titles!

Python as a High-Level Language

It would take several books, (perhaps an entire library), to explain exactly what Python is and how it works. However, our aim here is to provide you with enough information to make you curious, especially in the context of using Python for one of the most exciting developments currently worked on in the technological universe: machine learning.

At a very, very broad level, Python is related to C, C++, Java, and Pearl, all of which are high-level programming languages. However, this particular programming language brings improvements into the landscape and complements the other ones in the, "making of," complex software programs that push the boundaries of what technology can and cannot do.

All high-level programs have to be processed before they can be run on computers, as most of these machines only, "speak," low-level languages (also referred to "machine languages").

The fact that high-level programs have to be processed before they can be run on computers is one of their disadvantages. However, the advantages tend to outweigh the disadvantages:

- It is easier to write high-level language code

- It takes less time to write high-level language code

- High-level language codes are easier to read and they are shorter (also, they are more likely to be correct)

- High-level languages are more versatile, as they can be used on different types of computers with little to no modification (low-level languages cannot do this, as they have to run on one type of computer only and they have to be actually rewritten to work on another type of computer)

These advantages make high-level languages more likely to be used by programmers, while low-level languages are normally used by just a few applications. There are two types of programs that can process the high-level languages and make them readable by normal computers: interpreters and compilers.

Interpreting programs can read high-level programs and execute them, doing what the instructions on the program say. The way it does this is by reading one line at a time and performing the necessary computations.

Compiling programs can read the high-level program and translate them before they start running it. Once the high-level program has been compiled, you will be able to execute it again and again without needing to translate it again.

Python programs use interpreting programs to be executed and they do so in two main ways: through the command line model and through the script mode. In the first case, the Python program is typed and the interpreter will print the result. Working this way is usually convenient for both program development and testing, mostly because you can type out the programs and then have them executed instantaneously. Furthermore, once you have a working program, you should store it as a script and execute/ modify it at your own will in the future.

So, What Is a Program, Anyway?

If you have ever used a computer, there is no chance in the world you missed the term,, "programs." Chances are, if you are reading this book, you are at least vaguely familiar with programming in general and this is not the first time you have heard about "programs," (or even Python).

However, for the further understanding of what Python is as a *program*ming language, it is necessary to go back to the roots a little and provide a basic explanation of what programs are and how they work. Regardless of whether the concept is only vaguely familiar to you or if you have tons of experience in other programming languages, it is important to go through these basic (and maybe slightly boring), concepts once again.

So, a program can be defined as a sequence of instructions you write in order to specify, (to a computer), how to run a computation. It can be something mathematical, such as solving an equation, or it can be something symbolic, such as searching/ replacing a chunk of text in a document.

Different languages will use different vocabulary, syntax, and grammar to create the details of how a program is built. However, there are some instructions common to most of the languages used by programmers:

- The program input method (you can get the data from a keyboard, a device, or a file)

- Display the data on screen (or forward it to a file/ a different device)

- Math (performing basic math operations)

- Ensuring certain conditions are met

- Executing the right sequence of statements

- Performing some actions repeatedly (with some sort of variance)

Sounds simple, right?

Most people think of programming as a very intricate procedures - and while it may not be easy, especially at very advanced levels, programming is nothing more than writing a series of instructions computers can read and understand, using a language with its own vocabulary, syntax, and grammar.

Programming breaks large tasks into smaller tasks until they can be performed according to basic instructions. That may be, perhaps, why project management styles like Scrum are very popular in software development companies - they break down the large tasks into smaller ones the same way a programmer breaks down the tasks a program has to run into smaller ones.

Smash That Bug!

Needless to say, real-life insects have nothing to do with programmers - but hiccups in any program can be terribly bugging, both for the end users and, sometimes, for the programmer himself/herself as well.

Programming is very human. Yes, programs may be run by computers - but, until some sort of Skynet-like AI is developed (hopefully never *that* way), behind all those endless lines of codes lie engineers who are, at the end of the day, *human*. So, they are prone to making mistakes and errors.

That's where the debugging process kicks in. To ensure a program is fully functional and useful for the end users, the programmers are usually backed up by an adjacent team of quality assurance specialists who spot bugs and point them out to the programers to be squashed. The debugging part falls into the lap of the programmer(s) who wrote the code in the first place - and it is an extremely important part of your job because it will allow you to make sure all your programs are running correctly.

There are three main types of errors that can occur in any kind of program:

1. *Syntactical*

In Python, a program can only be executed if it is syntactically correct (if it isn't, an error message will be returned). In basic terms, the "syntax," of a code, is consisted from the structure and the structural rules of a program.

Compare this with English. In the English language, you must always begin a sentence with a capital letter. Exceptions are works of literature or poetry where the author intentionally chooses to start without a capital letter because it sends a specific message across).

When you write a sentence in English, you don't get an error message back when you make a syntactical error. However, not the same is true for Python. If an error occurs in the code, Python will send you an error message and it will not be able to run your program.

That's good news, actually, because it means that you will know you have made a mistake when you do it, and your programs will not run in a faulty way. Yes, you will most likely make plenty of syntactical mistakes when you start out with Python - but, same as with English, you will get better at this with practice.

2. *Runtime*

There are some mistakes that lead to so-called, "runtime errors." Unlike syntactical errors, these mistakes will not be pointed out until the program is run. Most of the times, these types of errors are very rare when you are a beginner in Python because when you are just starting out with this programming language, you will mostly work with simpler programs.

3. *Semantic*

After a short incursion into the more technical world of runtime errors, we return to more familiar grounds. In linguistics, semantics deal with meaning (word meanings and the relations between them). In logic, semantics deal with sense, reference, implication, and presupposition.

In programming, semantics deal with the meaning behind every instruction you give a computer. So, when you make a semantic error in writing the code, the program *will* run, but it will not do what you wanted it to do.

Identifying semantic errors is, perhaps, one of the most difficult things to do when debugging a program because you will have to run everything backwards and reverse-engineer your code until you spot that one mistake that made your program run differently than what you intended.

Debugging might sound awful (especially if you think of the concept of *bugging* things). However, once you grow accustomed to a programming language, you will find that debugging is one of the most challenging and interesting parts of your job. It is, in many ways, like playing detective against code bugs: tracking them, asking yourself the right questions, finding clues, and, eventually, finding a solution to solve the problem.

Chances are that you you will have to create several hypotheses and test them before you find the one that is correct and that will help you fix the bug in your program.

Debugging is, in itself, a form of experimental programming - and it should not be mistaken with the actual quality test. A programmer might not be the one who runs quality tests (since a QA specialist will most likely deal with this), but the programmer will always be the one to experiment with several solutions to find the right one.

Ideally, the debugging should happen as you go - so, whenever you finish one part of your program, it will be completely functional up to that point.

The Relationship between Language and Programming Language

As mentioned above, programming and playing with words as a writer are very similar in many ways: they both use semantics to convey meaning, syntax to provide structure, and they both want to send a message. In the case of written communication, the message is addressed to another human being (or a group of them). In the case of programming, the message is an instruction addressed to a computer.

The main difference between programming languages and, "human" languages lies in the fact that the first are formal languages, while the latter are natural languages. In other words, "human" languages are natural - they occurred naturally, nobody, "manufactured" them. Programming languages, on the other hand, were created by humans - ergo, they are, "formal."

Programming languages are not the only formal languages out there. For instance, the specific symbols and notations used by mathematicians is also a formal language created to denote the different relationships between numbers and symbols. Likewise, chemists use a formal language of their own.

Because they are man-made with very specific purposes, formal languages tend to be quite strict about rules - particularly syntax rules. Without these rules, these languages don't make sense. While you might have flexibility on how to play with words and their order in English, for example, and still be able to convey some sort of meaning, this is not true with formal languages.

Take, "$1+1=2$", for example. In mathematics, this is a correct statement. However, should we modify it into, "$1=/2$", it would not make sense. Likewise, "CO_2" is used in chemistry to name carbon dioxide, but you were to call it, "$2cO$", it would not make sense anymore.

There are two categories of syntactic rules:

1. Tokens: the very basic elements of a language (words, chemical elements, etc.)

2. Structure: the way the elements (tokens) are arranged

Going back to the analogy made with, "human" languages (as we called them above), if you write a sentence without the correct tokens or structure in it, it will not make sense. The process through which you figure out the structure of the sentence is called, "parsing."

For example, take the sentence: "I like *The Lord of the Rings* more than *Harry Potter.*" More or less consciously, you will parse this sentence and determine that "I" is the subject, "like" is the predicate, and, *"The Lord of the Rings"* and *"Harry Potter"* are complements. You may not consciously split the sentence into its basic elements, but parsing will help you extract the meaning out of the sentence, (assuming that you know what the two titles are all about, of course).

Formal and natural languages have, as shown above, plenty of things in common. However, they are very different as well, and the main features that distinguish between them include the following:

- Ambiguity (natural languages can be very ambiguous and they can rely on contextual information, while formal languages are almost always unambiguous)

- Redundancy (to reduce any kind of misunderstandings, natural languages are very frequently redundant, while formal languages are more concise)

- Literalness (natural languages employ idioms and metaphors that change the meaning of the statements, while formal languages only mean what they say)

Most people use the aforementioned features of natural language without realizing they do. You don't have to be a writer to use an idiom in day-to-day discussions, and you don't necessarily have to be a poet to say that you, "feel blue."

Programming as a formal language, however, does not come naturally to humans (just like any other formal language doesn't). This is why it is important that you practice and over-practice everything you learn in terms of formal languages - regardless of whether it's mathematics, chemistry, or programming.

Some of the things you can do to find it easier to read programs and other formal languages include the following:

- Accept that it just takes more time to read formal languages, precisely because they are denser than natural languages.

- Remember that the structure of the language is crucial, so you cannot read it from top to bottom, for example.

- Keep in mind that details can make a huge difference. Sometimes, a mistake as small as a punctuation mark or spelling issue can make your program faulty. This kind of mistakes may not be a huge deal in natural languages, but when it comes to programming and formal languages, they can completely turn your efforts upside down.

Hello, World!

"Hello, Word!" is the simplest and shortest program written in any language.

This is not a piece of information new to anyone who has dealt in programming before, and it might not be new for most of the people outside the realm of programming as well.

What might be new, however, is that, "Hello, World!" can actually prove that Python is extremely simple to understand and that once you learn the basics, the world is your oyster. To sum it up, in Python, a, "Hello, Word!" message displayed on screen is the equivalent of *print, "Hello, World!"* in Python. Of course, the quotation marks will not be displayed on screen - they just mark the beginning and end of a value, same as <> and </> mark the beginning and end of a value in HTML.

Python - The Connecting Bridge

Very often, Python is used as a connecting language - meaning that it can connect different components of a software application (and it helps with doing this in a flexible, seamless way). Furthermore, Python is also used as a, "guiding" language (because the Python modules can be used to control the operations at a lower level).

Python is an excellent choice for everyone, even those who are completely new to programming - and these days, it happens quite often that Python is people's first programming language. There are two main reasons for this: Python is relatively easy to learn because it's very logical and clean and, at the same time, Python can be a, "gate" towards the more sophisticated programming languages out there.

In many ways, Python is a simplified version of C and Pascal. In fact, it's so easy to understand that even someone who hasn't seen a line of code in their entire life will be able to make sense of what Python is, "saying." There are no awkward and odd symbols used in Python (no curly brackets, no dollar signs and no tildes). The indentation rules are easy and they limit the likelihood of bugs generated by this kind of problems.

Compared to other easy scripting language (scalable Unix scripting languages, for example), Python can handle more tasks, more efficiently, without complicating the script and allowing you to reuse the code. Python is *scalable* and modular - you can plug in new components by simply using the codes you already have. Even more, this programming language will allow you to split the code in different modules and reuse them in any other Python program.

Python will allow you to use standard modules, which can be used in other Python programs. Furthermore, Python will also allow you to use other programming languages within your program. For example, if you have to write a complex passage in C and you are not that familiar with this programming language, Python can help you.

Python allows you to use complicated expressions easily, using a single statement. For instance, this programming language will allow you to use lists and dictionaries (resizable arrays, respectively hash tables) without variables and without argument declarations. Once a value has been assigned to a name, this programming language will automatically assume everything correctly. This will all minimize the time and the amount of effort a programmer needs in order to implement functionalities in a program. The code size itself will also be reduced, thus making it more readable and easier to understand by whoever dives into it.

Other programming languages are more complex, especially since they require certain data structures and pointers. Plus, Object Oriented Programming is mandatory in programming languages like C, but it isn't in Python (it can be useful, but you can still use the language without it and learn OOP later on).

Even so, Python is a genuine object-oriented language, as all of its components are objects and you can even create class hierarchies based on these objects. Moreover, every object attribute has a name attribute notation. At runtime, the attribute is determined in a dynamic way.

Python is polymorphic in the sense that callable objects accept different types of arguments (optional, keyword, etc.). In this paradigm, one operator can have a variety of meanings, depending on the elements that are referenced. This is precisely why complex operations can be implemented using short Python declarations

Another feature that makes Python easier to work with is the fact that, when interpreted, it can support a byte compilation. This means that Python programs can run, can be debugged, and can be tested through the Python interpreter in an interactive way.

There are many other intricacies of the Python programming language that make it a genuinely good choice for beginners and advanced programmers alike. The same features make Python a nearly indispensable component of machine learning programming, pushing the three-decade old programming language into the future of computational technology.

I will not lie here: Python is not as easy to learn as any foreign language. To be able to, "speak" Python, you need to build a solid ground on what it is first and how it works - but maybe even more than that, you need to change your mindset and create the kind of thinking processes that allow you to communicate with computers. Both of these, "fundamentals" behind Python are the main goals of this book - so stick through it and you will definitely become more familiar with Python, especially in the context of machine learning and deep learning.

Python: A Modern Solution

Python is very frequently used these days for all the reasons explained in the previous parts of this chapter - but if we have to nail down one feature of Python that makes it very popular with programmers of all kinds, it's the speed at which you can code in this language. Python is, after all, officially classified as a rapid application development (RAD) - so it bids well that it fits into an age of tight deadlines and high productivity.

Moreover, Python is quite powerful (you can imagine that, given that it is used in machine learning developments) and very clear. Most often, Python glues together the smaller pieces of a large software application. It's used on various platforms, in middleware products, as well as application domains. It has the main role of integration of design in large applications that will be used for a long period of time.

Even more, if user requirements change, Python allows developers to rapidly change the code.

The market needs Python developers on a constant basis - so if you need any kind of motivation to get your hands dirty with this programming language, this should be strong enough (aside from the fact that data sciences and machine learning are pretty exciting fields to work in, of course!).

Despite its fame and its wide usability, Python is not difficult to learn - and the elegance and simplicity of its codes make it a top choice for many programmers, as well as software companies.

Chapter 2

The Absolute Basics of Python

It would be pointless to push you into a pool of Python concepts without teaching you to swim first.

And in order to swim in the pool of (very rich, mind you!) Python concepts, you must first become accustomed to its very basics.

Python has many features, indeed. But that should not scare you off - as explained throughout the first chapter, Python is truly one of the easiest programming languages to learn (and even complete beginners can grasp its intricacies quite quickly).

Programming from Adam and Eve

To understand how Python works, you first need to understand how programming works. We took a short dip into the waters of programming in the first chapter, when we explained what a program actually is - but in this chapter, you will learn the basic "rules" that govern the world of programming (regardless of the language you may choose to use).

Programming Is Not Computer Operation

It's one thing to start up your computer and pretend you're working while browsing through eBay's latest offers and it's a completely different one to start up your computer and *code*. The difference lies not only in the amount of actual work involved, but on how you use the computer itself.

Most people these days can use a computer for basic operations. Fortunately, software is getting easier and more user-friendly every day, so even complex tasks can be handled much easier than what they used to be back when computers were not as popular.

However, not everyone can code a software - not because people do not have the capacity to do it or because you need to be some sort of genius to do it (not in *any way* like that), but because most people don't speak the programming languages.

Software programs are, in many ways, translators that help the average user interact with the unknown, nearly magical inner works of a computer. So, as a software programmer, you will have to meta-translate everything in computer languages (Python, for example).

When you are coding a program, you control the computer. The results of your control may not always be what you expect, but even so, a second, third, or fourth attempt will definitely get you there.

When you work on a computer, you may sometimes feel that both of your computer and your work are being controlled by malicious little dwarves living in the electricity lines that fuel your office.

As a programmer, however, you will move past this lack of understanding and you will soon start to see why some computers and some programs run as poorly as they do (spoiler alert: most of the times, it is all about building software on top of software on top of software, all of which are unreliable in nature).

Programming Is Not Engineering Per Se

OK, so we have established computer use and computer programming are extremely different.

Another important thing you should understand before you delve into the world of coding is that programming is not actual, hardware engineering. It may come as shocking to you, but many programmers don't have much knowledge on how RAM memory sticks are built or how the intricate process of building CPUs has evolved in the past two decades. That's for hardware engineers (and, perhaps, hardware aficionados who consume every little piece of content under the Sun on how all of this works)

Programming in many languages might need you to have a solid engineering background - but when it comes to Python, you don't need that, as this is an interpreted language. In other words, there will be no endless sequences of 0s and 1s in your future and no Matrix-like rows of codes that make no sense whatsoever.

Python will allow you use actual words, but in a language that is simplified, a language that can be understood by everyone. As I was saying in the previous chapter, even someone who has not read a line of Python in their lives will still be able to make sense of Python.

Unlike English (or any other, "human" language), Python does not have the complexities of communication with other humans. Computers don't get metaphor, they don't use connotations, and they aren't moody - so once you have mastered the language to speak to them, you will be able to get them what you want them to do (even if it takes multiple attempts).

Sure, the software programs we all use these days are complex - but behind all those fancy features, computers and the programming that makes them run have not changed *that much*. They have become faster in terms of hardware and they can do a lot more in terms of software, but even so, the basics are still pretty much the same - in a similar way, cars are pretty much the same as they used to be when they first came out too.

Programming Has Remained and Will Always Remain Consistent

There is one not-so-secret secret computers and computing have used to stay as similar to their great-grandparents - and that is consistency. For you as a programmer, this means that you should always give very specific instructions for a program to do what you want it to do. Without these instructions, a program will not arbitrarily decide what to do.

Moreover, programs do not decide whether or not they want to do something. It might be like this with humans who have their own willpower and conscience - but, thankfully, computers don't. Sure, you have probably seen a zillion movies describing artificial intelligence that has become self-reliant and makes decisions of its own (most are related to bringing mankind to dust). But even *if* this is possible (because there is a tough debate there), we're still a long way from that. And no, as a programmer working with machine learning, you are not enabling this in any way. We will discuss more about this towards the end of the book, when we will tackle machine learning, what it is, and the benefits of using it.

Back to Python, though. One of the reasons that makes it so common in large software programs is because it allows developers to create very well defined and well behaved blocks of code. These blocks of code are professionally referred to as "objects" (and Python is, as mentioned before, an object-oriented programming language).

Good Programming Leaves Room for Changes

The main advantage of using object-based programming languages is related to the fact that you can easily puzzle them together and make them work. If you want to remove a particular feature or incorporate a new one, this object-based philosophy will allow you to easily do it without modifying the rest of the code that is not related to that particular feature.

Another concept you should understand is that programs should be able to adjust to real-life changes. Building a software that doesn't adapt to real-life needs means building a software that will have short-termed life in how many people use it. Like it or not, real life needs change - and your programs absolutely need to be able to adjust to these new situations. For you as a programmer, this means that your job is never fully done - which is both an advantage and a disadvantage. On the one hand, it means that even after a software is delivered/ put in use, you will still have work to do. On the other hand, it means that you should get accustomed to the idea that there is no such thing as a, "perfectly crafted program", precisely because it will have to adjust to some sort of change sooner or later.

Python is an excellent programming tool when it comes to all these needed changes because it will allow you to create programs that actually explain the user what failed in the operation they wanted to run and why.

Programming Is Fun

It really is. No matter what your professional background is right now, you can definitely rely on the fact that programming is fun. It is the combination between speaking a different language and interacting with "someone" who will always do what you want them to do (provided that you give them the right instructions).

That doesn't mean that accidents don't happen. They do. Even the most seasoned programmers make coding mistakes that crash software and make it, if not completely unusable, then at least faulty.

The First Steps in the World of Python

If you have ever learned a foreign language, you most likely started with some sort of manual (or, in more modern days, a software application).

In Python, aside from the actual manual(s) you will use, you will also have to set the, "landscape" that will allow you to communicate with your computer (I bet you always wanted to do this, right?).

Find Your Python a Home

The first thing you have to do is find a home for all the awesome codes you will write from hereon. In other words, you should find a Python code editor. At first, you will want something simple, as you will most likely not want to create complex programs right away. So, you won't need much else other than the Python Shell or IDLE.

As you become more experienced, you will want to search for a code editor that is a bit more intricate and allows you to play around with more code without losing its direction and meaning. There are two categories of code editors you can look into at this point: the ones dedicated specifically to Python and the more general code editors that allow you to work with more than just Python. The first category usually comes under the name of, "dedicated code editor", while the latter is usually called an, "IDE" (or, "Integrated Development Environment").

IDEs will normally include the following:

- Code editor (with features like syntax highlighting, for example)

- Tools that allow you to build, execute, and debug code

- Tool(s) to help you control the source code

Because IDEs are meant to support multiple types of programming languages, it might take a little longer to download them, as well as to install them. Also, since they are complex, you might need to be more advanced in the art of programming to operate them correctly.

Dedicated code editors, in the other hand, can be extremely simplistic. They can be simple text editing tools with code formatting and syntax highlighting features incorporated in them. Furthermore, they will also come with some form of debugging controller and code execution features as well. Due to the simplicity of these little programs, they are usually easier to download, install, and operate - so they might be the best choice for someone who is still a beginner in programming with Python (or other programming language, for that matter).

Just like we like our coffee differently, different programmers like different code editors. As you become more experienced in this, you too will start to grow, "favorites." Until then, however, there are some features you should probably look after when it comes to your editor (because these features will just make your learning process and your work easier). The features to look after include the following:

- The ability to save code files

- The ability to reload code files

- The ability to run your codes right from the editor

- Some sort of support for debugging (such as being able to go through the code as it runs)

- The automatic highlighting of syntax

- The automatic formatting of your code

These are, so to say, the bare necessities of a good code editor. As you become more experienced in programming with Python, you will most likely start to search for other features as well - but for now, anything that meets the aforementioned criteria is good enough.

Understanding Strings

Just like words are the basic unit in written communication, the basic unit of text when editing in Python are *strings*. One characteristic that makes strings different in Python (as compared to other programming languages) is related to the fact that, in Python, one letter can be considered to be a one-letter string.

In Python, strings are marked by quote symbols. Because quote symbols are used in normal, everyday English (and any other language), you will have to tell the code editor that you are talking to it, not to the humans who will eventually use your program. To do this, you will have to use what is called an, "escape character." In Python, the escape character is a backlash, "\" . So, if you have to use quotes for the actual text displayed on screen to the end user, you will also have to use a backlash to tell the editor that you are changing the addressee of your communication.

Aside from the concept of the escape character, there are some basic rules to using strings in Python - and the most important ones are the following:

1. Accessing substrings. Because Python does not support the use of a character type, these are usually treated as strings and substrings. To obtain a substring, you should slice the index you are trying to substring by using square brackets.

2. Python allows you to change an existing string by assigning (or reassigning) a variable to a different string. The new value can be completely new (a different string entirely) or it can be connected to its previous value.

3. Escape characters differ according to the non-printable characters you want to bring forward. Some examples include:

   - \b is used for backspace

- \cx is used instead of control-x

- \e is used instead of escape

- \s is used instead of space

- \t is used instead of tab

4. There are some special string operators that will allow you to work "magic" in Python:

   - + is used to add the values and connect them together (for instance, if, "a" is, "Hello" and b is, "World", a string consisted of a+b will print, "HelloyPython").

   - * is used for repetition (so a*4 will display, "HelloHelloHelloHello")

   - [ ] is used to slice, to give you the character from a specific index (so a[1] will display, "e" on screen)

   - [:] is used to slice from a given range (so a[1:4] will print, "ell"

These are just some of the basic special operators, and they can be used in a variety of contexts to help you write code that does more (and makes more sense).

5. There are also some string formatting operators you will use on a frequent basis. The most important one is %. Used in

different combinations, it will do different things, for example:

- %c is a character

- %i is a signed decimal integer

- %o is an octal integer

- %x is a hexadecimal integer

- %e is an exponential notation

6. There are some other symbols used in Python strings as well, such as, for instance:

- * is used to specify width and precision

- - is used for left justification

- 0 is used to pad with zeros, from left (instead of using spaces)

- <sp> is used to leave a blank space (when you need it before a positive number)

7. Triple quotes are sometimes used in Python. They allow different strings to span across more than one line.

8. Python also allows you to use unicode strings, which will allow you to use more types of characters (including characters used in some languages around the world).

9. Last, but not least, a very important thing you should know about strings is that this programming language has specific built-in string methods, such as:

   - capitalize() will capitalize the first letter of a given string

   - center (width, fillchar) will return a string with space pads, which contains the original string centered to specific width columns (as per the instructions)

These are all just examples of how strings are used and the specific terminology you should use when writing them - there is a lot more to Python strings than these examples. The main goal here was to show you how strings work, so that you gain a better understanding of how Python programs are built. As you learn specific string commands and as you learn to connect the strings, you will become more experienced at this and you will not have to check endless tables to make sure you are using the right operators, symbols, and the right methods.

The essential to remember here is that strings are the basic unit to work with in Python - and there are specific rules on how to do this coherently, in a way that will eventually help you pull together actual software programs.

The novelty of all of this may scare you a bit at first - but don't worry. Just like with any foreign language (or any kind of new learning process), it takes a bit of time to assimilate the rules. The key lies in practice, though. There's no point in learning Russian characters if you don't learn how to use them in actual practice, in words, sentences, phrases, and paragraphs that come together to have meaning.

The following chapter is dedicated to helping you learn the equivalent of "grammar" in Python: the way different elements are connected to create meaning (i.e. to create functional programs).

Chapter 3

How to Organize Python Elements into Programs

By this point, you might feel a little confused - and that's perfectly normal, given the amount of information you are getting familiar with right now. However, it is important to stick through with it and come back to each of the concepts in this book to deepen your knowledge.

The good news is that the way you organize python elements into programs is pretty easy to understand - mostly because, unlike other programming languages, Python uses actual English keywords very often (while other languages might use punctuation, for example).

The rules of Python are definitely different from those of the English language, but this is one of the closest programming languages to actual, "human" language. Therefore, as mentioned before, Python is a good way to start your programming journey.

This chapter will discuss some basic concepts behind the organization of Python elements into actual programs. Don't worry if you don't get it right the first time - come back to this information and deepen it using more advanced sources of information whenever you need to. The key is to be consistent with your learning - so dedicate a given amount of time every day to perfecting your Python knowledge (preferably, at least 30 minutes/day).

Indentation

Unlike other programming languages, Python uses actual whitespace indentation (while other languages might use curly brackets to keywords to make the delimitation between different blocks). There are specific statements you should use to increase the indentation of a block, and an indentation decrease represents the end of the block you are currently on.

Control Flow and Statements

Some of the most common statements in Python include the following:

- Assignment represented through the *equal sign* (=) token. This is one of the most important statements in Python and it is quite different than other, programming languages. In C, for example, if you say x=2, it will translate into "typed variable name name x is associated with a copy of the given numeric value 2). In Python, however, x=2 will translate into, "name x is referenced to a separate and dynamically allocated object of numeric type of value 2."

- *If*, which will execute a code block in a conditional way. This is usually used in combination with *else* and *elif* (meaning else-if).

- *For* , which is used to iterate objects that are iterable and allowing you to capture each element to a given local variable.

- *While*, which is used to execute a code block only if its condition is true

- *Def*, which defines a method or a function

- *With,* which allows you to enclose a block of code in a context manager

- *Assert*, which is used during the debugging process to check any conditions that have to be applied

- *Import,* which is used to import modules with variables or functions that can be used in the program you are working on

Expressions

In this respect, Python is quite similar to other programming languages (e.g. Java and C), but there are still some differences that should be noted, namely:

- Subtraction, addition, and multiplication are the same in Java, C, and Python, but the way the divisions behave is different (in Python, there are two of these: floor division and integer division.

- == is used to compare by value, while in Java, it is used to compare numerics by value and also to compare objects by reference.

- "And", "or", and, "not" are words used in Python for the boolean operations (while in other languages, "&&", "||", and, "!" are used.

- In Python, anonymous functions can be implemented by using lambda expressions. Still, these are quite limited because the body is just one expression.

Methods

In very short terms, methods are applied on objects and they are considered to be functions that are attached to the class of that object. The basic formulation upon which methods are built is "instance.method(argument)." This syntax is considered to be "syntactic sugar" (a method that allows you to do something easier) for "Class.method(instance,argument)."

Also, it should be mentioned that Python methods usually have an explicit self-parameter used to access instance data. On the other hand, other object oriented programming languages use the implicit self for the same purpose.

Typing

Before we dive into this area of Python, we should first mention that everything said here refers to Python 3 (and there might be differences between Python 3 and other versions of Python).

Python uses something called, "duck typing" - or, in other words, typing that is done according to the saying, "if it walks like a duck and talks like a duck, then it must be a duck." Simply put, in Python typing, what you see is what you get.

Python also comes with typed objects, but its variable names are untyped. When used, type constraints are not checked during compilation. If operations on an object fail, it means that specific object is just not of a suitable type.

Python forbids you from using operations that are not very well defined - such as adding a number to a string. Other programming languages, on the other hand, will attempt to make sense of operations that are not well defined.

As a Python programmer, you can define your own type using something called "classes" (mostly used in object-oriented programming). When you want to create a new instance of classes, you do this by calling the class (e.g. "SpamClass()") - and these classes become instances of the metaclass type. This allows for reflection and metaprogramming.

In typing, Python uses basic C arithmetic operators ("+", "-", "*", "/", "%"), it uses "**" for exponentiation and, starting with Python 3.5, matrix multiply, "@" will be used as an operator as well.

In Python, Boolean expressions can be used. To define these, Boolean expressions are logical statements that can either be true or false. In Python, Boolean expressions are used with equality relations in a way that is similar to their general use in mathematics.

Creating Functions

When you want to create a function in Python, all you have to do is write, "def" at the beginning of one line. This is a keyword - and your code editor will color its font with a specific color. Once you have written, "def", you can start to create the function by typing its name.

For instance, if you want to create a simple function, you will write, "def simple (parameters)." Some functions don't have parameters and they work very well like that. With more complex coding, however, you will have to use the right parameters according to the precise instructions you want to give the computer.

While parameters are not absolutely necessary with some types of instructions, the colon at the end of the function *is* very important, so make sure not to forget it.

When a function grows longer, it is not recommended that you continue on the same line. On the one hand, this will go against the good readability principle of Python. On the other hand, this will also go against good collegiality principles (meaning that you want your workmates or whoever you work with to be able to read your code well - and cramming endless functions on the same line is not how you do it).

Once you have created the premise, the function that will define the action you want the computer to take, you will also have to describe said action. For instance, if you want the computer to display text on screen, you will write, "print "insert here my first text in Python.""

Once you have defined this, you must call the simple function - or, in other words, to ask it to do its main job. To do this as per the example used here, you will have to write, "simple" (the name of the function to call) and add round brackets after that (" simple ( ) ").

Alright, this is your first, (very) simple function.

If you want to add a parameter to your function, you have to use specific language. For instance, if you use, "plus_ten" as a function name with, "a'" as a parameter, it will show, "10" as a result.

It is also important to return the value from the function as well. Otherwise, the function will simply print text instead of do a specific calculation, for example. To do this, you will have to write, "return" on the second line of the function (just like you did with, "print" in the aforementioned example).

Once you have typed the function, don't forget to call it as well, by using round brackets and the argument of your choice (e.g. "plus ten (5)" will return, "15" on screen).

When you define a function, you use a parameter. However, keep in mind that when you call that function, you are using not a parameter, but an argument. So, in the aforementioned example, you have, "called plus ten with an argument of 5."

Furthermore, it is also important to keep in mind that a lot of people mistake, "print" and, "return" a lot. To explain this a little better, here is an example. Let's say that you use argument, "x" as an input in a function (e.g. "x plus 10"). In this situation, "x" is an input, a value you already know, so combining this with the function will give you an output value (which we will refer to as, "y"). In programming, "return" is all about the value of, "y", or the equivalent of pressing the equal sign on a basic calculator.

While functions can take multiple inputs, they can only return one output that might be composed of one or more values. Therefore, "return" can only be used once in every function.

Because Python is an intuitive language, it sometimes allows you to use different names for the same function (for instance, "plus ten" can be replaced with, "addition of 10") without altering the correctitude of the function. Furthermore, you can assign more than one name to a function, as you see fit. This is advantageous because you will not have to call functions by naming and numbering them (x1, x2, x3), which might make your colleagues unhappy because they will find it difficult to make sense of what happens in that code.

When you name Python functions, you should make sure they are very clear and concise, as this will make your codes easier to understand.

Function in Function

In Python, you can also have function within a function.

To explain how this works, let's use a classic wage example. Define a wage function (that calculates your wage in a day) and use a parameter for working hours (you are paid, let's say, $10/h). When you define this type of function, you don't have to print it right now - you can just return your value for now and print it later.

Let's say that your company is willing to pay you a bonus of $10 if you perform well in a week. To write this in Python, you will have to define a function within a function - a, "with bonus" function this time. As a parameter, you should use working hours again. This large function will have two arguments: the one for your wage and the one for the bonus you will be paid when you perform well. The two functions are written and returned one underneath the other on the coding file.

To actually run the operations, you will have to input a line that looks somewhat like this: "wage(8), with_bonus(8)." The output line will display, "(80, 90)."

Conditional Statements

Together with functions, conditional statements are crucial in Python (and they are extremely commonly used).

The most basic conditional statement is, "if (expr) :" followed by, "(statement) on the next line, where, "(expr)" is an expression evaluated in the context of Boolean expressions and, "(statement)" is a Python statement that is both valid and indented.

If (expr) returns true, then the (statement) will be executed. If the (expr) returns false, then the (statement) will not be executed. As with functions. the colon after (expr) is mandatory.

If you want to evaluate a condition and do more things if it is true, then you will have to construct your conditional statement in a way that makes the computer understand that all the (statement)s you will list down should be considered as one block from a syntactic point of view. For instance, if you want to create a conditional statement that says, "if I am hungry, I will go to a fast food, eat a burger, and drink some soda", you will have to make sure the computer understand all the, "statements" (go to a fast food, eat a burger, drink some soda) as part of the same syntactic unit.

Different programming languages do things different ways - but in Python, it is all about the indentation of the code lines, a rule that is also known as the, "off-side rule." Basically, in Python, if two or more lines have the same indentation, they are considered to be of the same block (or suite) and the entire block will be executed if the (expr) is true (respectively, the entire block will be skipped if the expression is not true). The end of the block is denoted by a line that has a smaller indentation than the other lines of the block.

To execute your statement, return to a lesser indentation and, "print" the statements.

Keep in mind the fact that blocks can be created at arbitrary depths as well. This means that every indent will define a new block while every outdent will end the preceding block. This structure will allow you to create code that is intuitive and consistent.

Functions and Conditional Statements

Alright, so we have learned about functions and about conditional statements - but how about bringing them together? This is a very important concept to learn with every programming language, so do make sure to give it the attention it deserves.

Let's say that you have made a bet with a friend who doesn't believe you can save money. He said that if you will save $50 by the end of this week, he will top it off with another $25.

In Python, this would translate as a function (we will call it, "add 25") with a parameter, "m" (that changes according to how much you saved).

So, your function will say that if, "m" is greater than 50, the program should add another 25 to the total saved amount. If, "m" is lower than 50, the program will print a message saying, "You have lost the bet." In actual code, this will look something like this:

```
def add_25(m):

    if m >=50:

        m = m + 25

        return m

    else:

        return, "You have lost the bet"
```

If you have saved $49 and want to see what the program will show you, you will have to enter a new line and write:

add_10(49)

The output will say:

"You have lost the bet."

As you can see, everything in Python is very logical, once you learn the actual language and learn how to pull together the different components of the language.

Working with More Parameters in One Function

To enter more parameters in a Python function, you should enlist all the arguments, using parentheses, and separating them by comma.

This is very simple, but one thing you should definitely keep in mind is that you should pay attention to the order in which you call the arguments/ parameters (which should be the same as the one listed).

The only situation when the order does not matter is when the parameters are very clearly defined within the parentheses (for instance, "a=1, b=7, c=9").

The Import Statement

The modularity and flexibility of Python are two of its most commonly praised benefits. And they are sometimes materialized through something called, "the import statement" - a Python statement that allows you to use any Python source file in another Python source file. To use this statement, you will have to type, "import module" and the name of that module. The module will be imported from the search path - a list of directories the interpreter will use to search for an input to import a module.

To find the module, the interpreter will first search in the current directory, move to each directory in PYTHONPATH, and then it will check the default path (which might vary, according to the operating system you are using).

The PYTHONPATH is considered to be an environment variable that contains a list of directories.

Scoping and Namespaces

In programming, variables are defined as names (also known as, "identifiers") that map to objects. A namespace is a collection of variable names (also known as, "keys") and the objects that correspond to them (also known as, "values").

Variables are accessed through Python statements in a local namespace or in a global namespace. If the two variables have the same name, the local one will shadow the global one.

By default, Python assumes that any variable with a value assigned to it in a function is local. If Python has to assign a global variable in a function, you, the programmer, will have to use the global statement first (namely, "global VarName", which will tell Python that it should stop searching among the local namespace, and start searching globally.

The "dir()" Function

This function will return a list of strings that contain the names as they are defined by a module. The list will include all the module names, all the variables, and all the functions as they are defined in a module.

The "reload()" Function

When you import a module into a script, the code at its top-level portion will only be executed once.

So, if you want to want to execute the top-level code once again in a module, you will have to use the, "reload()" function, which will import a module you have imported before.

Python Modules

In very simple terms, a Python module is a file that contains Python code. The code can define classes, functions, or variables, but it can also contain runnable code.

Modules are easy to recognize because they are files with a .py extension. The name of the module you use in the code is also the name of the file, so this will be very easy to use.

There are three main ways Python modules can be used. They can be written in Python, they can be written in C and then imported in Python (to be run dynamically at runtime), or they can be intrinsically built into the interpreter.

Python Packages

Packages are structures of hierarchical file directories that define single Python application environments. These application environments are consisted of modules, sub packages, sub-sub packages, and so on.

Packages are crucial in working with machine learning projects, as you will later on see in the book - and the very best thing about them is that once you understand how Python works, you can just jump in an use the packages features. This means that you can get right in the middle of the machine learning action even if you are a beginner in Python.

Every Python package is a directory and it absolutely has to contain a file called _init_.py. This file might be empty sometimes, but it indicates that the directory is a Python package and it can be used the same way as a module would be used.

This chapter's main aim was getting you familiar with the inner works of Python. Hopefully, I managed to do this. Of course, these are the absolute basics and some of the most commonly used Python, "tricks" and code rules, but there are many others.

The important thing right now is that you shouldn't feel overwhelmed by the large amount of information you are acquiring right now. If you were to learn Spanish now and someone would start their first lesson with tenses, personal pronouns and genders in Spanish you would feel confused too (even if they would just brush over these areas of the Spanish language). However, if you were to go in-depth afterwards with all those concepts, taking them one by one, you would soon enough speak Spanish (provided that you practiced it as well).

Chapter 4

What Is Artificial Intelligence?

Of all the buzzwords that have flooded the mainstream landscape in recent years, artificial intelligence is, by far and large, one of the most fascinating and, at the same time, one of the scariest concepts.

Let me expand a little on this. Undoubtedly, artificial intelligence is incredibly fascinating - it is, in the end, mankind's chance to create something that mirrors it in the best of ways, just like a child mirrors his parents' genetics. Sure, there's an ethical debate on how artificial intelligence should be built in a transparent way that only follows humanity's best interest at large.

As for, "scary", artificial intelligence can qualify as such only as long as your reference point is Science-Fiction literature and cinematography. Sure, it is perfectly understandable why people would be slightly scared by the thought of artificial intelligence that will eventually exceed mankind's abilities. However, reality is far from SF scenarios - and artificial intelligence is here not to push mankind into its own demise, but to push us forward.

To help us be healthier. Happier. More productive.

Eventually, maybe, to reach stars farther and farther away from our own Solar System.

To push the boundaries of what we are and what we can do.

Artificial intelligence is, without doubt, a very complex field - but this chapter's main purpose is of showing you the very basics of what artificial intelligence is and how it connects with the main topic of our book, *deep learning* (which, we have to re-emphasize, is not the same as machine learning and not the same as artificial intelligence itself).

So, What Is Artificial Intelligence?

Sometimes referred to as, "machine intelligence", artificial intelligence is popularly defined as a machine's attempt to mimic the cognitive functions of the human mind - such as problem solving and learning, for example.

The exact definition of what AI comprises is actually very flexible - mostly because the more advancement is made in this field, less, "intelligent" tasks are considered to be actual artificial intelligence. This is an interesting phenomenon referred to as the, "AI effect."

So, if, let's say, we consider a robot that runs your house cleaning chores to be AI today, it might not be considered actually AI four or five decades from now, when this will become the norm (in a hypothetical scenario, of course, don't put off your house chores just yet).

Even with the ever-changing definition of what is and isn't artificial intelligence, there are a few areas that are generally considered to be part of the AI capabilities:

- Human speech understanding

- Strategic game competitions (such as chess, for example)

- Self-driving cars

- Military simulations

Obviously, the applications of AI span much wider than these four main fields - but, at the moment, they are the artificial intelligence industries that are more developed.

There are three main categories of AI systems:

- Analytical (AI that has acquired cognitive intelligence based on past experience learning)

- Human-inspired (AI that has acquired cognitive and emotional intelligence, is capable of telling human emotions from each other *and* is able to run cognitive processes to make the best decisions)

- Humanized (AI that has acquired social intelligence in addition to the cognitive and emotional one, is able to be self-conscious and self-aware in all its interactions with humans and machines alike)

Clearly, this last category is what Hollywood has been talking about - and it is, by far, one of the least developed and most complex areas of artificial intelligence, a sort of, "final frontier" of the AI world.

Artificial intelligence has walked a long and winding road to modern days. Established as an actual academic discipline in the mid-1950s, AI quickly lost funding interest after a series of disappointments, only to rise from its own ashes again and find new, exciting approaches that eventually attracted new funding.

The Current AI Landscape

At the moment, the world of AI research is very much split between a multitude of subfields. Most often, these subfields do not communicate with each other - and this is mostly related to the technical differences (e.g. some subfields deal in robotics, while others deal in machine learning), tool usage differences (e.g. some fields use logic, while others use artificial neural networks), or even philosophical differences.

On the one hand, this means that you shouldn't hold your breath before you get your own robot maid like the Jetsons. On the other hand, it also means that if you get into artificial intelligence now, there's a very good chance that you will have plenty of work to do in the next few decades.

There are several goals AI is looking to accomplish:

- Reasoning

- Planning

- Learning

- Knowledge representation

- Natural language processing

- Processing

- The ability to manipulate objects.

All of these goals come under the umbrella of, "general intelligence" - and, as mentioned before, most of them are treated as separate subfields, frequently not communicating among themselves.

On the other hand, AI manages to bring together specialists from areas that frequently did not communicate with each other either: computer scientists, IT engineers, mathematicians, psychologists, linguists, philosophers, and so on.

Artificial Intelligence Approaches

Because it is a fairly new field and because there is still a lot of work do to before we get our hands on the first, "movie worthy robot", artificial intelligence currently lies at the confluence of multiple approaches. Sometimes, they are used in combinations, other times, these approaches come as opposites on the research spectrum. All of them together, however, push the boundaries of artificial intelligence and everything it means.

The main AI approaches include the following:

Brain Simulation + Cybernetics

This is one of the first approaches taken in the world of artificial intelligence - and one of the biggest disappointments too. Created at the end of the 1940s and all throughout the 1950s, this AI approach brought together neurobiology, information theory and cybernetics. However, this direction in artificial intelligence was abandoned towards the 1960s, only to come back to light in the 1980s. In some ways, this, "primordial" AI approach is closer to what modern day artificial intelligence research focuses on than many of the other approaches that came after it.

Symbolic AI

One of the main directions in the history of artificial intelligence research was all about symbol manipulation. According to this approach, all human intelligence can be connected to symbol manipulation - and thus, it can be mimicked by machines the same way.

The symbolic AI approach eventually overshadowed cybernetics and artificial neural networks in the 1960s and gave birth to a series of sub-branches, including:

1. Cognitive simulation (trying to simulate the techniques used by people to solve problems)

2. Logic-based (trying to simulate the essential reasoning and problem-solving)

3. Anti-logic (also known as, "scruffy", an approach trying to demonstrate that logic cannot be applied as the general principle behind AI due to the complexities of areas like natural language processing)

4. Knowledge-based (trying to bring together the aforementioned approach by admitting that large amounts of

knowledge have to be fed into artificial intelligence systems even for the simplest applications)

Sub-Symbolic AI

By the beginning of the 1980s, people started to lose faith in AI symbolic systems and saw them as simply unable to imitate the cognitive processes of the human brain.

And thus, the original views on how AI should function, based on cybernetics, came back to light and breathed life into what is now known as sub-symbolic AI. In its own turn, sub-symbolic AI has given birth to a series of sub-fields:

1. Embodied intelligence (split between embodied, behavior-based, situated, and nouvelle AI, mostly focused on robotics)

2. Computational intelligence (based on neural networks and on the idea according to which some problems cannot be solved with absolute logical certainty)

Statistical learning

Soon enough, researchers realized that sub-symbolic AI is not necessarily enough for the creation of properly functioning artificial intelligence systems. So, the field of AI started to adopt sophisticated mathematical tools to both compare and combine different competing architectures. Because mathematics is more of a universal language, it allowed AI to communicate with other fields of expertise, such as operations research, for example.

Compared to the previous approaches, statistical learning was finally yielding actual results in very practical domains, like data mining). These artificial intelligence systems were not gaining any kind of semantic understanding of the datasets fed into them - but for the first time, artificial intelligence was starting to be perceived as scientific.

The most modern approach brings together everything that has been learned so far and is aiming to eventually bring together the different, divergent, and somewhat chaotic sub-branches of the artificial intelligence world.

Only future can tell on what will happen next in artificial intelligence research - but the industry is here to stay and major advances are made every day. While you might not be able to Netflix binge while a robot is handling your mail, dishes, and laundry, we're making slow steps in that direction.

If you're curious to stay in touch with the latest developments of the AI world, I strongly recommend you subscribe to YouTube channels like Boston Dynamics and see just how much robotics has evolved in the past few years. In parallel, artificial intelligence systems are now able to write poetry and (ironically enough) science-fiction stories. So yes, we're not that far from the, "AI dream" as it might seem - and being part of this world will surely bring you major satisfactions over the years to come.

Chapter 5

What Is Machine Learning?

Machine learning is a science that uses algorithms and statistical models to allow computer systems perform tasks without actual instructions, by relying on the induced patterns and the inference instead.

Machine learning is, as you will see, *not* one and the same with artificial intelligence. In some ways, the two are related and it would be futile to talk about one without taking the other one into consideration.

Machine learning algorithms are built on mathematical models, which, in their own turn, are based on sample data. This sample data is professionally referred to as, "training data" - and it is used to feed machine learning programs and enable them to make predictions and take decisions without being specifically programmed to do this.

Most of the times, people associate, "machine learning" with all-powerful machines that target mankind's well-being. Beyond science-fiction, though, machine learning has very practical applications - many of which you are probably using without fully realizing it as well. For instance, some email filters use machine learning. And so does computer vision. Furthermore, computational statistics is a field very much associated with machine learning in the sense that it too uses statistical data to make predictions using computers.

Other fields associated with machine learning include mathematical optimization and data mining (which is actually a subset of the machine learning field of study which focuses on using unsupervised learning to produce exploratory data analysis).

All in all, machine learning is a fascinating industry that is currently growing at an incredibly fast pace. As a programmer, you can find your niche in machine learning (and Python is one of the most common languages used here, especially in deep learning, as you will learn later on in the book).

Machine Learning Beyond Science-Fiction

Learning is a process human's are very much accustomed with. From the very second you breathe the air of this world, you learn to accommodate to it. As we grow older, our learning processes slow down (which is one of the reasons older people find it more difficult to accommodate to new technologies, for example). But even so, learning is part of who we are - as individuals and as a species.

Machines are not as futuristic as one may think. Mankind has been using various types of machines ever since the industrial revolution, when a lot of manual tasks started to be assigned to them.

The study of machine learning, however, is a bit more recent. The term itself was used for the first time at the end of the 1950s, at IBM, but the idea of, "teaching" machines how to learn had started to take shape at the beginning of the decade already. In 1950, famous Alan Turing tested a computer, curious to see if it could fool a human into thinking he was talking to another human. In 1952, Arthur Samuel wrote the very first program to resemble machine learning in the more modern sense of the term - a game of checkers.

Needless to say, machine learning has grown a lot in the past seven decades, and it is currently pushing the borders of technology in a multitude of industries - including medical, cinematography, and everyday life. In fact, the machine learning industry is already present in nearly a quarter of the companies in North America, with 23% of the businesses here admitting that they use machine learning for a minimum of one company function. Numbers are a bit lower in Europe (21%) and China (19%), but all the data points in the direction of machine learning growth over the next few years.

Machine Learning: The Absolute Basics

It would be hard to fit everything machine learning is (or isn't) in one chapter - and even in one book. However, my aim here is to help you understand the very basic concepts lying behind machine learning, so that you understand how they tie into deep learning in general and Python deep learning in particular.

As it was also mentioned in the beginning, machine learning is a science that enables machines to learn on their own, based on experiences, observations, and patterns they spot in a given data. In this case, machines are not programmed to do these things every time they do it - they are programmed to be autonomous.

Machine Learning, Deep Learning, and Artificial Intelligence

To understand what machine learning is, we will put it in relationship to artificial intelligence and deep learning. These three fields of study are frequently intermingled - and thus, frequently misunderstood as being (more or less) one and the same thing.

However, as it was also mentioned before, they are not exactly the same.

- Artificial intelligence is the ability of a machine to mimic human behavior and take intelligent decisions like humans do;

- Machine learning is the ability of a machine to learn without being specifically programmed for it;

- Deep learning creates something called "neural networks" (which will be explained further on in the book). These neural networks have the capacity to learn and take intelligent decisions by using certain algorithms.

So, How Is It That Machines Can Learn?

It is quite obvious how humans learn, it is embedded in our DNA and it is the very motor of our ascension to the top of the food chain.

Machines can learn in a pretty similar way. At first, they receive knowledge about a given topic, so they are able to identify it in the future. Knowledge, combined with past experiences, help machines make decisions for the future. Just like humans, machines can be trained to identify features and patterns in the data they receive - and thus, they are enabled to make the distinction between various topics.

When data is fed into a machine, it will be divided into two main parts: training data and testing data. Once the data has been assimilated, the machine will learn to distinguish patterns and features and to train itself to take decisions based on the given data. It will be able to identify, classify and predict new data as well.

To make sure the decisions made by machines are accurate, the testing data will be used.

Let's say that you want to predict whether or not stock prices for a given company will drop in the next days. Traditionally, you would do this by collecting past information about those company stocks and present information, such as the situation of the company, the investments they made, technology they are putting forward, and so on. Based on this data, you will be able to make a more or less accurate prediction of what is going to happen.

In machine learning, you would do the same thing: collect the past and present data and feed it into the machine. Based on its programming, the machine will run an analysis of the patterns and it will predict the possible outcomes of the current situation.

Not only is it faster for a machine to make predictions, but chances are that, being a *machine* and not being influenced by emotions or "hunches", the predictions made by the said machine will be more accurate than those made by a human.

Machine Learning Algorithms

There are several types of machine learning algorithms, each with its own specificities

Supervised algorithms

In supervised algorithms, the data set that, "trains" the machine contains labelled data (meaning that it contains both the input parameters and the required output). For instance, if you want to classify persons according to the gender, "male" and, "female" will be your labels, and the training dataset will be classified according to these labels, based on specific parameters the machine will use to make the actual classification.

Supervised learning algorithms come under multiple typologies, including classification algorithms, which are used to classify data into given classes and labels. One of the most common classification algorithms is the K-Nearest Neighbor (also known as KNN) classification algorithm. This type of algorithms is used to classify a data set into given groups or classes based on the main similarities found between the data points in the set. For instance, if you need to check if a person is fit based on their height and weight, you will use this kind of algorithm.

Unsupervised algorithms

This type of algorithms works with unlabeled data, which means that when a machine is clustering the data into a specific group, it will do so based on the similarities shown by different variables.

Some of the most common unsupervised machine learning algorithms include K-means clustering.

Clustering is the forming of collections of data points which are brought together in groups created based on their similarities.

In the case of K-means clustering, "K" is the number of centroids to be considered for a given problem, while, "means" is the centroid at the center of any cluster.

To create this kind of algorithm, you will first have to define the value of K. If K=4, it means that there are four centroids. Then, you will have to select the K data points and check the distance between each data point and the centroids. Once you do this, you will have to assign the data point to the specific centroid that shows the shortest distance. This way, you will create the first cluster of data points that are similar.

You should then repeat the same process for each of the newly formed clusters, reassigning the data points to the centroid that can be found at the smallest distance from a given data point.

The number of iterations depends on how many times you have to repeat the process until the centroid stops changing. Once you see that it has remained the same, your algorithm can be considered to be fully optimized.

Reinforced algorithms

Reinforced algorithms are used to teach a machine to determine the best behavior given a specific context.

This type of machine learning works based on the principle of reward and punishment. This means that every decision taken by the machine will be either rewarded or punished. Based on this system, it will understand if a decision was correct or not. Eventually, the machine will learn to take decisions on its own, for the purpose of maximizing the reward long-term.

How Is Machine Learning Used?

Contrary to the popular belief, machine learning has nothing evil in it (that's just the result of several decades of Hollywood movies infused with end-of-the-world scenarios).

By this point, machine learning has touched pretty much every industry: from medicine to gaming and from agriculture to social media. Some of the most common utilizations of machine learning can be spotted in the following areas:

- Virtual assistants (intelligent assistants, for example)

- Social media (sentiment analysis, for example)

- Transportation (air traffic control, for example)

- eCommerce (product recommendation, for example)

- Healthcare (disease diagnosis, for example)

- Financial (fraud detection, for example)

Every area of human life can be improved by machine learning. From the way your favorite animations are made to the way surgery is done, machine learning has entered our lives. More often than not, their presence in our lives is more or less invisibile, in the sense that there are no trumpets to announce the fact that a company is using machine learning tools to make your experience better.

But they are. And chances are that this trend will continue to grow, to the point where most of the things in our lives will be carefully filtered through intelligent machines capable of simply making everything easier, better, more efficient, and more accurate.

Aside from the fact that this means there's a huge market for data scientists, it also means that you have the chance to work in an industry that is genuinely exciting. You have the chance of building a better, safer, more efficient future - and that should be a powerful motivator behind your own learning process.

Chapter 6

What Is Deep Learning?

As it was mentioned before, deep learning and machine learning are two different concepts. They are, indeed, very much related and they both pertain to the larger family of computational intelligence - but knowing the difference between machine learning and deep learning is really important, especially if you want to work in any of these fields.

Deep learning pertains to the larger field of artificial intelligence, yes, and it is a subfield of machine learning itself. However, deep learning is not necessarily, "AI" in the generally accepted terminology (it does not aim to mimic human behavior), and it is not, "machine learning" either (as it uses a completely different approach in generating solutions to problems that are frequently different than those machine learning is working with)

Deep learning is all about algorithms that are inspired by the very structure and function of the human brain. These algorithms are called, "artificial neural networks."

Because it is the kind of field that is moving at a very high pace, deep learning is frequently defined and redefined according to different perspectives. As you have read in the chapter related to artificial intelligence, the parent science behind deep learning is being constantly redefined as well - so it makes sense that something that springs from it will follow a similar pattern.

Deep Learning and Neural Networks

Artificial neural networks lie at the foundation of deep learning in its modern understanding. Google itself uses large neural networks for Google Brain, one of the most impressive advances made in the field of artificial intelligence in general and deep learning in particular.

Unlike machine learning, deep learning uses the structure of the brain to be able to make learning algorithms easier to use and more efficient, as well as make excellent advances in the AI and machine learning industries.

Deep learning could not have developed earlier than it has - mostly because it is only now that we hold the necessary hardware to perform deep learning activities and train neural networks of large dimensions. The amount of data fed into these systems is tremendous and it would have been simply unfeasible to think about it a couple of decades ago.

Even more, neural networks continue to grow with every training process, and their performance grows exponentially as well. On the one hand, this means that we are finally able to create scalable AI efforts. On the other hand, it also means that the hardware requirements are extremely sophisticated - so, going back to the main idea, it is only now that the world is fully prepared to embrace deep learning with all its power.

Machine learning reaches a plateau in the learning process at some point - but deep learning goes far beyond that, continuously growing and expanding over its own limits. Both supervised learning and unsupervised learning have their own applications - but right now, deep learning looks like the AI branch that will help the most in terms of building a, "true" artificial intelligence system.

The very name of the, "deep learning" science points out to just how grand it is, with, "deep" signifying the number of learning layers. And with this being a scalable effort, the efficiency of these systems will just get deeper and deeper as time goes by. The more data these systems are fed, the bigger their models are, and the more computational power is added to these systems, the better the algorithms will become.

This is very similar to how humans learn. The more you accumulate knowledge and data in a particular field, the deeper you can go in it. Just think of yourself reading this book as a complete novice to the Python and deep learning world.

At first, you started off with a very vague idea of what both Python and deep learning are. The more you progress with your reading, though, you assimilate more information and you are ready to go more in-depth with everything. Once you finish the book you will (hopefully) be able to deepen your knowledge in these topics - and the more advanced you get, the easier it will become to acquire new and complex concepts and apply sophisticated strategies.

Deep Learning and Feature Learning

Scalability is not the only benefit of the deep learning science. Another very important advantage to point out is deep learning models' ability to extract features from raw data. This process comes under the name of, "feature learning."

Beyond neural networks, deep learning systems can discover and acquire as learning good representations - and they use feature learning to do this.

Deep Learning and Its Deep Meaning

As I was briefly mentioning above, the very name attributed to the field of, "deep learning" bears with it important significance and downright philosophical implications.

"Deep learning" could have very well been referred to, "artificial neural networks" and the definition would not have been very wrong. That is the very foundation of deep learning, in the end - so why not call it as it is and use a fancy name instead?

Well, it can all be drawn back to Geoffrey Hinton, one of the main pioneers in the world of artificial neural networks and the man who participated in the creation of the first paper on training perception networks on multiple layers. He is frequently referred to as one of the first researchers to use the word, "deep" in the description of artificial neural networks - and his description seems to have stuck with both the research world and the media.

Using the, "deep" adjective to describe these, "greedy" neural network algorithms makes all the sense in the world. The, "depth" is all about the multitude of layers in these algorithms, but, at a philosophical level, it is also about the large amount of information machines can process and learn using deep learning algorithms.

Deep Learning in Analog Domains

While other forms of machine learning may be excellent for information that comes in tabular format, deep learning is excellent at solving problems where inputs and outputs come in an analog format (like pixel data, text data, or even audio data).

This means that the information fed into deep learning systems does not have to be pre-processed. Deep learning is able to make sense of complex information, just like the human brain is.

This is not to say that all deep learning systems can do this - but there are some, and they are quite impressive at what they do (especially given that they will continue to self-grow over time). A very good example in this direction is the object recognition network architecture at Facebook. Yann LeCun, the director of Research at Facebook, is also the first to have developed the Convolutional Neural Network (CNN) by using multilayer perceptron feedforward neural networks. This technique allows the system to scale data and be trained with backpropagation.

Yann LeCun's deep learning system challenges the very definition of deep learning precisely because it has had great success at image object recognition. You may be familiar with it, actually: when you post a picture on Facebook, for example, the system is able to recognize not only where in the picture a human face is detected, but very often, it is capable of actually detecting *who* that human face belongs to.

DeepMind is another very good example. A company founded by Demis Hassabis and later on acquired by Google itself, DeepMind managed to successfully combine deep learning techniques and reinforced learning. This technique has led to the creation of systems capable of playing complex strategies games like Go.

While the definitions, approaches, and techniques employed by deep learning may be vastly different across different schools of thought and they might vary even from one researcher to another, one thing is for certain: deep learning is here to stay, same as machine learning and artificial intelligence.

In very simple terms, deep learning systems are large neural network systems that need a lot of data and a great computational power to yield excellent results, particularly in problems that machine learning is limited to.

The main algorithm lying at the basis of modern and forward-thinking deep learning programs is backpropagation, represented through a series of popular techniques:

- Convolutional Neural Networks

- Multilayer Perceptron Networks

- Long Short-Term Memory Recurrent Neural Networks

This may all sound confusing - but the main purpose of showing you this is to make you curious. Deep learning is a fascinating world that brings together mathematics, computational science, programming, psychology, and much more - and all signs prove that deep learning will lay the grounds of a new era in the artificial intelligence field.

Chapter 7

Deep Learning Programming Concepts

So far, this book has been a preamble meant to show you just how intricate, fascinating, and absolutely rich fields of study Python and deep learning are.

As we are approaching the second half of the book, I want to introduce you to concepts that connect the world of Python and the world of deep learning - concepts which, I hope, you will assimilate with a thirst for information that will eventually instill in you the passion needed to go further with your study of using Python for deep learning.

There are a million reasons I would love for you to do this - but the single most important one is because *you opened this book for a reason*. You may be looking for a career change, or you may be genuinely interested in the world of artificial intelligence (and both Python and deep learning will open the gates to it). You may be an experienced programmer looking to grow in an industry that is taking over the future. Or you may be just a curious mind looking to learn more about the captivating world of robots and human-mimicking machines.

Regardless of where you stand, I hope this book will satisfy your thirst for knowledge and curiosity and that it will push you into further, deeper learning (pun intended).

The chapter at hand is meant to circle you back to the beginning of the book and show you how programming and deep learning connect in a network of information. I know there was an abrupt change between the first part of the book, focusing on explaining Python, and the second one, explaining artificial intelligence and deep learning - but if you want to stick through with this and continue to learn, this chapter will be the bridge you are looking for.

A Deeper Look into Deep Learning

When thinking of the human brain, a neural network is a system of layered neurons, with most of them having an input later and an output layer (at least). Deep learning systems mimic that, aiming to create computational power capable of imitating the way the human brain functions.

In deep learning, the program (yes, the one you will contribute to as a programmer) is the tool that will feed an input pattern into the input layer. Next, the output pattern will be returned from the output layer.

In between the input and the output layer, a series of processes happen - and, because they are very much misunderstood and debated, they are frequently referred to as the, "black box." Nobody knows exactly what happens in between the two layers of the human brain's neurons, but fortunately, we know enough to be able to imitate the same, "system" in man-made technologies.

Traditional Programming vs. Neural Networks Programming

Different architectures have different definitions on what happens between the input and the output layers - but if there is something consistent about all of the approaches is that you will have to express input problems as arrays of floating-point numbers (or numbers that contain floating decimal points). The solution to the input problem will also be an array of floating-point numbers.

Neural networks are only able to perform this kind of expression. They do not loop, they do not call subroutines, and they do not perform other tasks that are generally associated with traditional programs. In other words, neural networks simply recognize patterns.

Hash tables are the closest neural networks get to traditional programming. These tables map values between themselves, indexing different terms. In most cases, neural networks function the same way too. For instance, BAM (bidirectional associative memory) will allow you to provide a value and receive a key (the two basic concepts associated with programming hash tables). The value a hash table would return in traditional programming is the equivalent of the output layer of a neural network.

This is not to say that neural network programming is one and the same with hash table programming - the first are much more complex and sophisticated. For instance, if you input a word in a hash table that does not contain its definition, you will get a null result. On the other hand, a neural network will never give you a null result - they will simply search for the closest match. Even more, they will be able to modify the output in order to accommodate and estimate the value that was missing too.

For example, let's say you would input, "ate" in a hash table that does not contain the definition of the term. The result would be, as mentioned above, *null*. However, if you did the same with a neural network, it would probably give you results for, "eat."

One of the main challenges of neural network programming is translating textual or string values into floating-point numbers the neural network can understand. Some solutions have been developed, but even so, the principal challenge with neural networks remains the fact that it is easier for them to process numbers, rather than words.

One of the first operators you will learn in neural network operators is the, "XOR" one. similar to the, "AND"and, "OR" operators. In the case of an AND operator, both of the sides of the operation have to be true. In the case of an OR operator, on the other hand, one of the sides has to be true. And in the case of an XOR to be true, both of the sides of the operation have to be different from each other.

Supervised vs. Unsupervised Learning Programming

We have already touched upon the topic of supervised learning and unsupervised learning, but let's put it in the context of programming this time around.

When you, as a programmer, specify the ideal output, the machine learning you are using is called, "supervised learning" (i.e. you don't let the machine calculate whatever output may be, but make sure you give it instructions on what that output should be like). Supervised learning will teach the neural network/ the machine to produce an ideal output, as per your instructions.

When you don't specify the output, you are using unsupervised learning. This type of learning will teach the machine to group data according to the output neuron count.

Both of these types of machine learning are iterative. In the case of supervised learning, each of the training iterations will calculate how close the machine is to the ideal output (and this closeness will be expressed as a percentage error). With each training iteration, the internal weight matrices will be adjusted to decrease the error rate to a level that is as low as possible.

In unsupervised learning, the iterations will not calculate the error that easily, precisely because there is no ideal output the machine should target. Therefore, the iterations will have a fixed number, until the results are narrowed down to an acceptable level of error.

Getting Friendly with Algorithms

As a programmer working with machine learning, your main purpose is that of creating an algorithm capable of constantly improving itself based on the data that was fed into it.

The type of learning you need to use depends on a lot of factors, including the type of data you are handling. For instance, if you are dealing with tabular data, as mentioned in the previous chapter, you might find it better to work with a more traditional machine learning approach. However, if you are dealing with complex data, such as images, deep learning programming is what you are lookin at.

Furthermore, it is very important to note that even the best deep learning systems in the world have a marginal percentage of error. They may get *very* close to 100%, but they never reach that point. This means that whatever their outputs may be, they are not always absolutely certain.

Machine learning becomes useful in a very large number of situations. As a programmer, even if you are familiar with all the possible scenarios of an input output, there will (almost) always be a very large number of variables you cannot humanely calculate. In these cases, machine learning comes to complement traditional computer programming and allows you to create an approach that will eventually return solutions that are as close to absolute accuracy as possible.

The precise type of algorithm you will use also depends on the type of data you have to work with. For instance, if your data is unlabeled (each row of information does not have any kind of label associated with it). In these cases, clustering of data will occur (you will group together elements or data points that have some sort of similarity to each other). This type of algorithm could match any new input to one of the clusters the machine has already created, without knowing exactly what that information represents.

If the data is labelled (i.e. each row of data is associated with a specific label), your job as a programmer will be to ensure the machine can give outputs that have a low rate of error.

In reinforced learning, the machine will learn from reinforcements that come with the data and its main goal will be to achieve the objective you set for it (the point with the highest reward). As a programmer, you will assign a positive reward score to paths that appear to be beneficial and negative reward scores to paths that appear to be detrimental. In this paradigm, the machine will do its best to find the path that offers the highest reward.

Same as real life, human learning, the best path to the highest reward might not always be the straightest one - and it may sometimes have to move through unsuccessful paths to reach the best one. In the end, however, the goal will be achieved.

As a note, some of the most commonly used algorithms associated with reinforced learning are Q-learning and SARSA.

Programming for deep learning follows the same basic principles as all programming does. Even so, it shows significant differences as well - so even if you are an experienced programmer, but you have never worked with machine learning before, you will still have plenty to learn.

The next chapter of this book will help you finally connect the dots that have been elaborated throughout these past several chapters. Hopefully, it will help you understand why Python is a good choice for deep learning, as well as *how* it can be used for deep learning (because, as it was mentioned in this chapter, neural networks deal better with numbers, not the strings of instructions so typical of Python). Believe it or not, though, Python is one of the easiest and most efficient programming languages for deep learning - and the next chapter will show you exactly why.

Chapter 8

Deep Learning with Python: Why, How, When

O nce upon a time, there was a great man who created a very straightforward and useful programming language. The time was 1991, the man was Guido van Rossum, and the programming language was Python.

Except for Alibaba, whose Jack Ma actually recorded their very first meeting, convinced this would be a historical moment, most of the businesses and inventions in the world did not start with a bang. Python makes no exception, as Guido van Rossum surely did not expect his little project would take on such a throw.

These days, Python is used in a number of applications, including fast prototyping. The reason? It is easy to understand, clear, facile in terms of formatting, and it helps you stay "clean" for later self and for your colleagues as well. So, it makes all the sense in the world that this language would be popular among those writing prototype programs that may or may not be continued right after their inception (and may or may not be continued by the same teams).

In fact, Python is one of the fastest-growing programming languages in the world, according to a study ran by StackOverflow. [2] Over the past years, it has managed to surpass in popularity programming languages that were far more common and older than it - such as PHP and C, for example.

Clearly, the benefits of Python are attractive for a wide range of programmers - from those just starting out in the world of programming and for the seasoned ones alike.

Beyond the simplicity and beauty of the coding style, Python wins your heart with its quirky style and with the whimsical way in which everything about it was constructed from the very beginning. If C is an elder with lots of knowledge, but no sense of humor, Python is a Millennial who has charisma and empathy for everything around itself.

What Does Python Have to Do with Machine Learning?

Pattern recognition lies at the foundation of most of the learning processes - it is what pushed humans into becoming Homo Sapiens and it is precisely the underlying concept behind machine learning as well.

----

[2] Stack Overflow Developer Survey 2018. (2019). Retrieved from https://insights.stackoverflow.com/survey/2018

At a very simplistic level, machine learning is nothing but the ability of a machine to recognize patterns in the data. So, as an engineer working in machine learning, your main tasks include:

- Extracting data

- Processing data

- Defining data

- Cleaning data

- Arranging data

- Understanding data

- Developing algorithms according to the aforementioned understanding of data

Given the fact that your main job is not so much related to programming per se, but to teaching machines by using a language they can understand, it makes a lot of sense that you use a simple programming language. And that is precisely where Python enters stage.

With complex linear algebra and calculus concepts used in machine learning programming, you want to minimize your effort as much as possible - and one of the very best ways to do this is by implementing your programming by using Python.

The Data Matters

Machine learning is all about data - the way it is structured, shared, grouped, and analyzed. However, data comes in a multitude of facets - images, video, language documents, audio files, and so on.

The, "thing" with data is that it rarely comes in a structured way - especially in machine learning environments, where the very nature of the industry is all about processing raw data. So, when you get all the information you have to feed a machine with, it will most likely be very raw, very unstructured, and, overall, *very bad.*

That is where Python kicks in to help. Because of its very organized nature, Python can help you organize the data you feed into machines - and there are multiple ways to do this:

Packages

Packages are a fundamental part of Python, and even more so when dealing with machine learning projects. The fact that there is a very large collection and stack of codes from various open sources is very helpful for programmers working with machine learning. These libraries are true gold for anyone who wants to create machine learning and deep learning programs and they can be excellent sources even for beginners.

Some of the most popular libraries include the following:

- For working with image data: numpy, opencv, and scikit

- For working with text data: nltk, numpy, scikit

- For working with audio data: librosa

- For working with machine learning problems: pandas, scikit

- For working with deep learning: tensorflow, psytorch

- For scientific computing work: scipy

- For those times when you want to see the data as clearly as possible: Matplotlib, seaborn, and scikit

- For web application integration: Django

All these libraries are filled with modules that can be easily installed in Python for your own use. Because they are open source, they are free to use in any context, adding even more benefits to Python programming.

If you are not comfortable using modules that have been created by someone else, you can implement their functionality from ground zero too. This might be a bit more difficult for a beginner, but it can definitely be worth it if you want to take up the challenge and make sure your codes are written by you from scratch.

The Speed Issue

Python has a long list of benefits that makes it grow in popularity from one year to another. At the same time, it would be unrealistic to say that Python holds absolutely no disadvantages - it does, and one of the most significant ones is because it needs a good system to be used. Both your processor and your memory need to be quite good to run Python properly - without these elements, Python will be slow because it takes too much space. C and C++, on the other hand, can work on less than great computers as well.

Some developers choose to implement neural networks in Python only for particular tasks, but still use C for deployment because it is faster. The great news? A mélange between Python and C is being developed (and it will be called, not surprisingly, *Cython*). This new programming language is meant to make things as fast as they are on C and as readable as they are on Python, bringing the best of the two worlds together.

How to Use Python for Deep Learning

There are, of course, specific techniques and tactics used in deep learning with Python - and while this section's aim is not to show you *all* there is to Python deep learning, it will hopefully show you some of the essentials you need to keep in mind should you proceed on this path.

Basic Data Structure

There's no point in trying to understand how Python works in machine learning if you don't first understand the basic concepts behind data structure. In other words, you have to understand how machines, "think" and how they perceive data in order to deliver the very best results.

It all starts with one byte - this is the, "atom" of the computer, the smallest unit based on which it can work. Every single line of code in the known Universe is written with this unit in mind.

There are several types of data structures:

1. Arrays - the most basic type of data structure, with linear arrays and one-dimensional arrays being the simplest. An array will always hold values of the same type (e.g. integers, strings, etc.). Also, you can quickly access the elements in an array.

   Furthermore, an array's size will always be fixed and it will be defined from the very beginning. Once this is done, you cannot increase its size without creating a new array that is larger and copying all the old values into the new array.

   Matrices are two-dimensional arrays (just like mathematical matrices are represented by two-dimensional grids). In some situations, you might find the word, "vector" used to refer to an array. However, this is not necessarily 100% correct, as tuples are a more correct mathematical concept to connect to arrays.

   In general, arrays are used for table implementations (more specifically, look up tables). As a result, people sometimes use the term, "table" as a synonym for, "array."

   Almost all programs created by mankind use arrays, as these are among the oldest and most common data structures.

2. Linked lists - sets of data that are linked together by references. "Nodes" is frequently the term used to refer to the data in linked lists, while the references are frequently called, "links" or, "pointers."

   In the case of linked lists, pointers are compared or dereferenced only for equality. As a result, linked data structures are very different in essence than arrays.

3. Stack - basic data structure defined by the fact that it can be logically conceived as a linear data structure that is represented by physical stacks or piles. Because it comes as a *stack*, any deletion or insertion of items can only be done at one end of the stack (called very intuitively "the top of the stack").

   To get a better idea of what stacks are, imagine an actual pile of books. You cannot take a book from the middle of the pile without crumbling the entire construction into pieces - so you can only remove them one by one when they are on top of the stack.

4. Queue - abstract data types that show the basic characteristic of having a first element that is inserted from one end of the structure (called the "tail") and having the deletion of an existing element from the other end of the structure (called "the head").

   To understand queues better, imagine people waiting in line for movie tickets. The first person there will be the one that buys a ticket, and the last person in the same line will be the last one to buy a ticket.

5. Graphs - abstract data types created with the purpose of implementing the eponymous concept from mathematics.

   Graphs are consisted of a finite set of ordered pairs (referred to as "edges") of nodes and vertices. Just like in mathematics, the edges are said to point from X to Y, while the nodes can be incorporated in the graph structure or act as external entities (which are represented by references or integer indices).

6. Trees - very advanced types of data structures, connected very tightly to artificial intelligence and design. Despite its advanced attributes, the tree is usually important in a very basic application - ensuring an efficient index.

   Trees and indexes frequently come hand in hand. Moreover, a tree will usually have a defined structure. If you have to use a binary tree, you can make use of a binary search that will allow you to locate any item in the tree without "manually" searching for it.

7. Hash tables - arrays in which every index is connected to a linked list. The connection is made based on a hash value, and a hash value is determined by a hash function.

Learning Python: More than Just the Basics

I am definitely not advising you to jump beyond the basics of Python if you haven't fully mastered those. You can probably move along more or less basic tasks without fully understanding the inner works of Python - but this will be short-lived. Plus, simply copy pasting code from the libraries poses a great risk of eventually leading to bugs you cannot remove on your own.

Practice makes better - it is a statement that stands just as true when it comes to Python learning as it stands true for physical exercise, mathematics, or even artistic endeavors.

The basics are meant to give you a solid jump start in the realm of Python and deep learning - but going beyond that and constantly practicing is the key to driving yourself forward, just like this entire industry relies on self-learning.

This entire book so far had a very clear aim: to introduce you in the world of deep learning via Python as a programming language. It is understandable how all the information here might be very new to you and how it might all feel overwhelming. Although we have barely scratched the surface, I do hope that all the tips and all the information here have made you curious.

I will dedicate the last chapter of this book to helping you understand the grandeur of deep learning - from its very incipient days to how it is constantly growing outside of its own shell in contemporary times.

Furthermore, we will discuss the ethical implications of artificial intelligence and deep learning, precisely because I am more than certain you have questions in that area as well. I am a firm believer in the power of ethics and in how they should shape the future - not just of deep learning, but of mankind as a whole. With deep learning (and artificial intelligence in general), ethical implications become all the more important, especially since there are a lot of people still fearful about the future of machine learning.

I hope you enjoyed your read so far - and I truly hope that my last chapter here will help you grow more curious and more avid for more and more information related to this fascinating field.

Chapter 9

The Future Is Here: Are You Ready?

Many of the things we are able to do today were mere science fiction at some point in mankind's history. Flying, for example, was considered to pertain to the realm of pure fiction back when Jules Verne was imagining worlds where people can travel around the world in a flying balloon. Clearly, if anyone had come forward back then and said that it *can* be done, people would have immediately classified that person as, "crazy."

Fast-forward just little over a hundred years and people can travel around the world by air for prices lower than they have ever been.

Up until not very long ago, machines capable of taking decisions and making predictions were, too, in the realm of science-fiction. Sure, there might have been a couple of, "crazy" people who believed it can be done - but for the largest part of the population, nobody imagined just how far we'd come in this field of science (and how little it would take for the snowball effect to kick in).

Like it or not, the future is here and soon enough, everyone will have refrigerators texting them to buy milk, clothes to automatically adjust the body temperature, and automatic cars to drive us everywhere we want.

The question lies not in whether or not these innovations will become the *norm*, but in *how* are we going to incorporate all these novelties in our lives in a way that maintains our integrity, our privacy, and our very hope for a better existence.

Data ethics and AI ethics aims to answer all these *how* questions. As a programmer, you might not care that much about ethics in general - but if you want to feel that you pertain to something grander than mere codes and a job that brings in a good paycheck, this chapter is for you.

Ethics may have nothing to do with programming - but when your programs have such a large impact on mankind as a whole, you definitely need to get accustomed to the best practices from an ethical point of view.

There are three main areas I want to tackle in this chapter: data collection, jobs, and the implications of the life-changing innovations brought in by deep learning. Before we get to those topics, however, I want to take a short trip back in time, to the beginnings of deep learning, and to show you how far we've come in this field of knowledge.

The purpose of these sub-chapters is not necessarily to give you lessons in history - but to show you that things are moving fast and the ethical implications of what we are doing today should move according to the evolution of deep learning and artificial intelligence. I want to show you that ethical issues have to be handled *now*, not at a later moment, because *now* is the right time for a field that changes drastically from one month to another.

Hopefully, this chapter will prove useful to you in two respects: it will make you curious about the fantastic field of artificial intelligence (and thus, more eager to learn its intricacies from the point of view of a programmer) and it will help you find your own, "place" in the grand scheme of things.

The History of Deep Learning

Although cutting-edge and futuristic, deep learning was not born yesterday. There is a long list of moments that led us to this particular point in time and space in terms of how deep learning has evolved over the decades.

Every time new discoveries are made in the realm of deep learning, massive disruptions occur in the world - particularly in the world of business, but in society and economy as a whole.

These days, deep learning is defined as a branch of machine learning capable of using algorithms for data processing to mimic the thinking processes of human beings (and even develop abstractions). As mentioned earlier in the book, deep learning uses different layers of these algorithms to pass the information through them sequentially (so the output of the first layer becomes the input of the second layer, and so on until the information has passed through all the algorithmic layers).

Deep learning was not always this sophisticated, though. It took decades before deep learning became this advanced - and it took decades before deep learning (and artificial intelligence in general) became accepted as a proper science.

The history of deep learning starts in 1943, when two great minds decided to create a computer model that was imitating the neural networks of the human brain. Wallen McCulloch and Walter Pitts made use of their mathematical and algorithmic knowledge to create this process.

Ever since that moment, deep learning has evolved year by year, at a relatively steady pace. There were two moments that marked the history of deep learning as we know it today. The first one was when, in 1960, Henry J. Kelley created a continuous Back Propagation Model. The same model was simplified by Stuart Dreyfus two years later, in 1962, which marked the second big moment in the evolution of deep learning.

Three years later, the first efforts to develop deep learning algorithms started to take shape, when Alexey Grigorevich Ivakhnenko and Valentin Grigorevich Lapa created polynomial model activation functions, and they were analyzed statistically.

The slow evolution and some of the disappointments connected to artificial intelligence set the industry back in the 1970s, when less funding became available for such endeavors. However, research continued, despite the lack of funds.

By the end of the '70s, another breakthrough took shape, when Kunihiko Fukushima designed neural networks that had multiple layers (both pooling and convolutional). The neural network created then came under the name of Neocognitron and it used a multi-layered, hierarchical design, which allowed computers to recognize visual patterns.

Back propagation was a major breakthrough in the deep learning field too. This technique allowed deep learning model training to use errors in their processes. In the 1970s, Seppo Linnainmaa wrote FORTRAN, a code for back propagation. Towards the mid-1980s, this concept started to be applied to neural networks as well.

Later on, in 1989, Yann LeCun made the first practical demonstration of how back propagation works, showing how this concept helped him train a machine to read the numbers on checks that were handwritten.

By 1995, the first vector machine support was developed, a system that was capable of recognizing and mapping similar data. Four years later, computers started to adopt GPU processing for deep learning. This pushed the entire industry a lot further, as the new computational capabilities allowed deep learning machines to process information at much higher speeds. The end of the 1990s was the beginning of a whole new era in deep learning and artificial intelligence - for the first time, the science-fiction dreams of the 1950s were becoming palpable reality.

Starting with the 2000s, deep learning boomed and evolved at a much higher pace. At the turn of the millennia, a research ran by the current Gartner (former META Group) brought forward challenges and opportunities for 3D data growth. This was the beginning of Big Data (although the concept has grown to be a buzzword only in recent years, its very beginnings are drawn back to that 2001 research paper).

In 2009, more than 14 million labeled images were used as inputs to train neural networks in an experiment called ImageNet. Due to the high increase in GPU power, there was no need to pre-train every layer of a neural network anymore - and this led to a faster and more efficient process that eventually allowed image data to be processed correctly, coherently, and speedily.

In 2012, Google Brain pushed deep learning even further with their Cat Experiment. This experiments goal was to explore the main challenges of unsupervised machine learning. More than 10 million unlabeled images were taken from random sources (including YouTube) and input in a neural network that spread across no less than 1,000 computers. That year marked the beginning of unsupervised learning in the fullest sense of the word.

As you can see, there is a snowball effect triggered by certain key moments in the evolution of deep learning. The more advances are being made, the larger the snowball becomes and the faster it moves towards the end goal. The beginnings of deep learning and artificial intelligence may have been slower and the industry may have even had some hiccups along the road - but with tech giants invested in this field, there is a very good chance that things will move even faster from hereon.

Like it or not, the world has to be prepared for, "true" artificial intelligence sooner, rather than later.

Deep Learning Applications

The greatest thing about deep learning, machine learning, and artificial intelligence is that it isn't just pure theory. These days, deep learning has very tangible applications that make it not only an interesting field to work in, but also a very generous one from the point of view of the job offers on the market.

There's nearly no field known by mankind that has not been touched by deep learning yet - and that can only be great news for someone like you, who wants to start programming machine learning.

Some of the most well-known deep learning applications include the following:

Automatic Speech Recognition

This is, by far, one of the most successful fields of deep learning. Large-scale automatic speech recognition machines can actually take very complex tasks (sometimes referred to as, "very deep learning tasks") that include speech events in multi-second intervals.

Who uses this?

Pretty much every single commercial speech recognition system in the world: Cortana, Skype Translator, Google Now, Baidu, Apple's Siri, and so on. All of these assistants are based on deep learning speech recognition - and they are used by millions of people around the world on a daily basis.

Image Recognition

Also, very impressive, image recognition based on deep learning has managed to become nearly superhuman, being able to produce results that are more accurate than those of actual human competitors.

One of the most interesting applications of image recognition in deep learning is FDNA (Facial Dysmorphology Novel Analysis), a machine learning tool that is being used to analyze human malformation connected to genetic syndromes.

Visual Art Processing

Visual art tasks have been touched by deep learning too. These trained machines are now capable of identifying the specific style period of a painting and apply it to any photograph to create imagery that is striking and resembles the stylistics of the original style period that was analyzed.

Natural Language Processing

This is mostly related to machine translation and language modelling, two fields that adopted machine learning as early as the first years of the 2000s.

One of the most relevant examples of how deep learning was applied in the field of linguistics is Google Translate. Although many would argue that the translations given by Google's translation tool are not accurate, the truth is that they have become increasingly better over the years. The reason they are much better now than what they used to be is because deep learning was used in Google Translate's evolution.

The large end to end long short term memory network employed by Google Neural Machine Translation learns from millions of examples that are fed into the system every day. This has allowed the tool to be able to translate whole sentences, rather than just pieces, thus helping users make a lot more sense from the translations given by this tool.

Customer Relationship Management (CRM)

Mostly applied in eCommerce and other similar business endeavors, CRM and deep learning connect over direct marketing actions that are generated by RFM (Recency, Frequency, and Monetary Value) variables. These machine translation tools allow eCommerce owners, for example, to create a better assessment of the customer lifetime value (and thus, make marketing and business decisions based on that).

Bioinformatics

Deep learning is also used in the field of bioinformatics, to predict gene ontology annotations, as well as the relationships between genes and functions.

Furthermore, deep learning has been used to predict the sleep quality of a person based on the data collected by some types of wearables (such as smart watches). The same principle is applied in predicting health complications based on the electronic health record data as well.

Medical Image Analysis

Healthcare and medicine reap a lot of benefits from using deep learning, including in the sub-branch of medical image analysis. More specifically, deep learning has shown impressive results in cancer cell classification, image enhancement, organ segmentation, and lesion detection.

Online Advertising

Online advertising (and more specifically, mobile advertising) also employ deep learning tools to find the right audiences to target in their ads. The reason deep learning proves to be very helpful in this field is because a lot of data points need to be taken into consideration, which makes proper online ad targeting challenging.

Financial Fraud Detection

Systems created for the purpose of anti-money laundering and fraud detection have been quite successful as well. These deep learning tools are capable of spotting and recognizing the relationships and similarities between different types of data, so that they eventually detect anomalies.

Of course, these are just some of the applications of deep learning. Every day, new deep learning systems are created for new fields of interest, helping humans achieve better results in their range of expertise. Lives are saved, people are entertained, businesses grow faster due to the emergence of these deep learning technologies - and, as I was mentioning earlier in this book, all research points out that the deep learning trend is only growing.

Consumer Goods

Machine learning uses natural language processing to create products that are, if not more useful, then most certainly more interesting for users. For instance, Hello Barbie is a doll capable of listening and responding to the kid playing with her.

Coca-Cola is using deep learning too. It might be surprising, since they are, after all, a soft drink company. The main way they use machine learning is by using the data they collect from the millions of buyers around the world to create new products and even create augmented reality machines in their plants.

Creative Arts

Watson, the famous IBM computer that won a *Jeopardy!* competition is now capable of helping restaurant chefs make the best food combinations to create the most unique flavors. This is, in itself, a form of art, proving that there *is* room for AI in art.

Furthermore, Watson has also helped human artists create works of art based on the history and culture of Barcelona and the style of Gaudi's work. The results are interesting (to say the least), as this is the first time artificial intelligence has been used for a purely artistic endeavor.

Last, but not least, Watson is also capable to process millions of data sources to inspire new songs by giving composers different musical elements to use in their work. In these cases, artificial intelligence helps musical artists understand what their audience likes (or doesn't like), so that they can create music that will be appreciated.

Energy

BP, the global leader in the energy industry, is using big data and AI to improve the use of resources. Furthermore, they are making oil and gas production and refining safer and more reliable for everyone.

Moreover, GE, another energy giant, is using the power of AI to create what they are calling a "digital power plant" - a power plant that is more efficient and more reliable in every respect.

Manufacturing

Many car manufacturers use data collected by their cars to predict when certain parts will fail (or simply when the cars need servicing). This makes cars safer both for those who drive them and for the other participants in the traffic.

Furthermore, many car manufacturers (including BMW) are using artificial intelligence to develop cars that are entirely autonomous and can be driven without any kind of human intervention.

Last, but not least, even the world of agriculture is touched by deep learning. Tractor manufacturers use artificial intelligence to provide farmers with better crop analysis, as well as the opportunity to automate many of the processes involved in farming.

Deep Learning Today, Day by Day

To help you understand just how deep the field of deep learning goes and just how much it has changed everyone's lives already, I will dedicate this section to showing you specific examples of deep learning and how it is used in its myriad of applications.

Keep in mind, this is not meant to advertise any kind of product or service, but to show you that deep learning is far more common than many people think and that it is not a field pertaining to the higher levels of each industry, but one that belongs to all of us to some extent.

So, without further ado, let's dive in:

Image Curation on Yelp

Although Yelp may not be as popular as it used to be, it still has a very important role to play in how people experience the new places in their living areas (or the different locations they visit as tourists, for example).

At first, Yelp may seem like anything but a tech company - but they are using actual machine learning to make sure their users come back to the site because it provides them with actual, helpful information.

More specifically, Yelp has developed a machine learning system capable of classifying, categorizing, and labeling images submitted by users - but more importantly, this system helps Yelp do this in a genuinely efficient way. This is extremely important for the company, given the huge amounts of image data they receive every day.

Pinterest Content

Who knew searching for wedding ideas on Pinterest is fueled by machine learning?

Pinterest's main purpose is that of curating existing content - so it makes all the sense in the world that they have invested in machine learning to make this process faster and more accurate for their users.

The system developed by Pinterest is capable of moderating spam and helping users find content that is more relevant to their own interests, their styles, and their searches.

Facebook's Chatbots

By this point, it is more than likely that you have stumbled upon at least one chatbot in Facebook Messenger.

These apparently simplistic chatbots are, in fact, a form of primordial artificial intelligence. Sure, Skynet is not typing from the other end of the communication box, but even so, chatbots are a fascinating sub-field of artificial intelligence - one that is developing quite steadily.

Facebook Messenger allows any developer to create and submit their own chatbots. This is incredibly helpful for a variety of companies that emphasize their customer service and retention, because these chatbots can be used for this precise purpose. Sometimes, Messenger chatbots are so well-built that you may not even realize that you are talking to a, "robot."

Aside from chatbots, Facebook invests a lot in developing AI tools capable of reading images to visually impaired people, tools capable of filtering out spam and bad content, and so on.

In some ways, a company that might not seem to have a lot to do with technological innovation is pushing the boundaries of one of the most exciting fields of the tech world: artificial intelligence.

Google's Dreamy Machines

Google is one of the companies constantly investing in artificial intelligence (often, with amazing results). Not only have they developed translation systems based on machine learning, but pretty much every area of their activity is somewhat related to artificial intelligence too.

Don't be fooled - Google has its hands in much more than search engines. In recent years, they have invested a lot in a very wide range of industries, including medical devices, anti-aging tech, and, of course, neural networks.

The DeepMind network is, by far, one of the most impressive neural network research projects ran by Google. This network has been dubbed as the "machine that dreams" when images recreated by it were released to the public, opening everyone's eyes to how artificial intelligence, "perceives" the world.

Baidu Voice Search

Since China is the leading country in artificial intelligence research, it only makes sense that their leading search company, Baidu, is heavily invested in the realm of artificial intelligence too.

One of the most notable examples here is their voice search system which is already capable of mimicking human speech in a way that makes it undistinguishable form, well, *actual* human speech.

IBM's Watson

We couldn't have missed Watson from this list, mostly because this is one of the first impressively successful artificial intelligence endeavors in history.

Most people know IBM's Watson from its participation in *Jeopardy!*, but the supercomputer built by the super tech giant IBM can do *much* more than just compete in televised shows.

In fact, Watson has proved to be very useful to hospitals, helping them propose better treatment in some cancer cases. Given the paramount importance of this type of activity in medicine, it can be said that Watson helps to save actual lives - which is a truly great example of how AI can serve mankind.

Salesforce's Smart CRM

Salesforce is one of the leading tech companies, specifically in the field of sales and marketing, where the tool helps businesses maximize their sales potential and close more deals with their customers.

Salesforce is based on a machine learning tool that can predict leads and assigns scores for each of them. For sales people and marketing pros, this is a true gold mine because it makes the entire sale process smoother, more fluent, and, overall, more efficient.

Where Do You Come From, Where Do You Go, Deep Learning?

Clearly, deep learning advances are quite fascinating. Many take them for granted simply because the speed at which they have developed in recent years means that every year brings a new tool to the market - a tool to use in medicine, healthcare, business, commerce, and more.

The future of deep learning cannot be predicted with certainty - if we had an ultra-powerful AI, it might be able to make an accurate prediction of what will happen next. Even so, *human brains* figure that the following will happen over the next few years:

Better Learning

The more they learn, the more powerful machines become. We have a long way to go before we see the first full AI that is capable of mimicking thought processes and emotions - but the more AI is learning, the faster it will continue to grow.

As I was saying earlier in this book, it is a snowballing effect - so the more the "machine learning ball" is rolling, the larger it will become, and the more strength it will have.

Better Cyber Attack Protection

While humans might be able to beat codes created by humans, it might be a little more difficult for hackers to break in when an AI is protecting the realms of data held by a company. Soon enough, artificial intelligence will be capable of better monitoring, prevention, and responses when it comes to database breaches, DDoS attacks, and other cyberthreats.

Better Generative Models

Generative models aim to mimic human beings as much as they can, in very specific areas. The Baidu example in the previous section is a very good indicator here. Over the next few years, we will start to see a lot more of these very convincing generative models, to the point where we will not be able to make a clear distinction between humans and machines (at least in some respects).

Better Training for Machines

Machine learning training is fairly new, given the rapid ascension of this industry in the past couple of decades. The more we train our machines, however, the better we will become at it - and this means that the machines themselves will be able to make better, more accurate decisions.

Deep Learning and Its Ethical Implications

As I was saying at the beginning of this chapter, it is important to discuss the ethical implications of machine learning - and more specifically, it is crucial that we discuss them *now*, as this is the moment machine learning is *happening*.

Postponing discussions in this direction can lead to nothing good - not necessarily in the sense that an all-powerful AI will overthrow us, but in the sense that all the amazing advances made in the field of artificial intelligence, machine learning, and deep learning might backfire against humanity in some ways.

There are *a lot* of issues to discuss in connection to the ethics behind artificial intelligence endeavors, but my aim here is to touch upon some of the most important ones. These are the problems that should be discussed both for their short term implications and for their long term ones - the ones that should lie at the very foundation of the future we are building for ourselves.

Algorithm Biases

No matter how amazingly well built an algorithm or machine are built, they are only as good as the data that's fed into them is.

If you are feeding your body junk food, your body will suffer and it will slowly start to function improperly (might happen sooner or later, but the effects of a poor lifestyle will eventually start to pop).

The same goes with algorithms as well - if you feed them low quality data, they will yield poor results. This means that even machines are biased, according to the data they work with.

Not only can this lead to low accuracy results, but it can also create situations where machines are fed with information that is unethical and/or immoral - such as racist data or sexist data). In these cases, machines would not be able to create results that are ethical or moral.

This happened, actually. For instance, some algorithms associated, "black people" with, "gorillas", so when someone searched for, "gorillas" in a search engine, the image results gave pictures of black people.

Obviously, this raises important ethical questions. What type of data should go into a machine? Who selects that data? Who selects the person who selects that data? Truly, artificial intelligence can build a better and more uniformly equalitarian world - but if the people behind the buttons are in it with their own personal biases, this could grow into a very significant ethical issue.

Algorithm Transparency

In some ways, deep learning machines gain a, "mind of their own" - not necessarily in the sense that they are uncontrollable (and will push all the nuclear buttons in the world at once), but in the sense that not even they can understand themselves.

When an algorithm is growing at a fast pace, it will develop inner methods that are obscure even to the people who created the algorithm in the first place. Thus, these machines will be able to make predictions, but they will not be able to explain their predictions.

This can have harmful implications in people's lives. For instance, if a company is using deep learning software to select which employees stay and which ones go when the business is reducing its manpower, the machine will output names based on an algorithm that does not explain its actual choice and does not take into consideration *humane* factors.

Where do we draw the line between accuracy and transparency and what should we focus on? Europe's GDPR is a very good example here, not necessarily through prism of the, "goodness" of the legislation itself, but through the prism of the fact that GDPR was born out of an ethical discussion: should accuracy be sacrificed in the name of transparency? Europe said, "yes", but what will other parts of the Globe say next?

Algorithm Supremacy

This is more of an apocalyptic scenario than I would like to bring into discussion, but where do you draw the line when it comes to the decisions algorithms make and the decisions humans make?

Even more, which of these parts will end up having the final say? Will it be algorithms because they are more accurate, or will it be humans because, well, they are more *human*?

This becomes increasingly important in situations where actual human lives are heavily influenced by the decisions taken by algorithms and humans.

For instance, there are some machine tools capable of deciding prison sentences. On the one hand, some say that this is a more accurate way to calculate what prison sentence a person needs to receive (precisely because humans have their own biases and they might be affected by a wide range of factors, including their mood on a particular day).

On the other hand, algorithms are only fed with statistical data, which might be biased themselves. For instance, machines might find a black person to be more likely to commit the same crime if their prison sentence is shorter, and they would be making this decision based on data that was biased to begin with. Given the fact that we have a history of racism, the machine would only be accumulating that and making decisions based on what mankind has done so far.

In this kind of situation, who should have the final say? A judge who didn't sleep well for the past three nights and might be seriously affected by this, or a machine that's been fed poor data?

Even more, what are the direct implications of choosing one option or the other? Will prisoners be able to appeal the decision because they were judged by biased artificial intelligence? What happens when racist machines make poor judgment calls - can they be, for instance, sued for discrimination?

Fake News

Jokingly or not, "fake news" is a term that has grown to be immensely popular since the 2016 US Presidential Elections. Beyond all the memes and the jokes, however, fake news are a really big issue - one that should be tackled once and for all.

Artificial intelligence is capable of pulling together all the information they have on a particular person and create fake stories about them, to publish them online and disseminate them to the world. Clearly, this can be heavily biased from multiple points of view - and, with a little help from an unethical programmer, it can lead to seriously fake news.

A similar issue appears when you consider fake videos. Some artificial intelligence systems are so smart that they can make it seem that a person is saying something in a video, when, in fact, they are saying something completely different. These systems are so seamless that they make it almost impossible to distinguish between a real video and a fake one.

This can be a major problem. Imagine the president of the United States of America appearing in a video, declaring that they will send nuclear missiles to Iran, for example.

At a smaller scale, given that videos can be faked to such a high level of perfection, how can they be admissible as evidence in court? And if videos aren't admissible, then what else can be more revealing and more realistic?

So, where do we draw the line between the real and the fake, the play and the terrifying reality? Who should monitor these things, how can users protect themselves from seemingly real news that is 100% fake?

Autonomous Lethal Systems

Deploying drones in wars seems to be a more humane approach towards the military who don't have to risk their lives in direct confrontations. Even more, these smart drones will be able to decide whether or not to kill someone without needing human approval.

However, this poses serious issues in terms of morality. On the one hand, it is clear that this kind of murder weapons can be incredibly dangerous - because, like all deep learning machines, they will just continue to self-improve to the point where they do not even need human direction. What happens, then? How do you stop them from killing random people, or how do you make them understand murder is immoral?

Even more, how do you prevent these weapons from being built at all? Will a ban on autonomous lethal systems actually stop them from being developed underground? And if that happens, isn't it better to allow them to be created and used above the ground, where they can be closely monitored and kept under control.

Autonomous Cars

Being driven anywhere without touching the wheel is a dream for many of you who might not be particularly fond of actual driving.

At the moment, there are no cars that are considered 100% autonomous, but even with the point we are at now, there are still some ethical questions that have to be answered before we let autonomous cars drive us everywhere.

For instance, self-driving cars have been known to kill pedestrians. Who is responsible here? The driver, who has been advertised that he can let the car do the job for hm, should it be the engineer who programs the machine? Should it be the company that manufactured the car?

Even more, if an autonomous car has the choice between driving into a truck or into a person biking on the side of the road, what will it choose?

These are, of course, very important questions. At some point, autonomous cars will most likely become safer than the average driver - but even so, what happens in those situations where the machine has to make a judgment call between two bad choices?

Also, once autonomous cars become the norm, should it be illegal to drive a traditional car, as a human?

The Thin Line between Privacy and Surveillance

It's one thing to know that your store or your house are equipped with high-end surveillance equipment that has the ability to recognize faces and it is a completely different thing for this surveillance equipment to be installed in public spaces, monitoring, without fault, every single move of every single person in a country.

It sounds like a scenario torn out of a dystopian movie, but Big Brother is closer to you than you may think. These equipment's exist and the idea of implementing them in public spaces exists as well. The motivation behind this makes sense, as it means that the citizens would be better protected.

What happens when surveillance trespasses the boundaries and becomes a major privacy issue? Again, where do you draw the line between protecting your citizens and following them around like an obsessed, abusive spouse?

Deep Learning and Data Collection

Without data, there is no machine learning, no deep learning, no artificial intelligence. But sometimes, the major questions lie not in the way we implement legislation that regulates the *use* of said machines and artificial intelligence systems, but in the way we implement legislation that regulates the data that feeds into these systems.

Obviously, this data comes from a variety of sources - and a lot of times, your very own internet activity is the culprit for a myriad of information you are feeding into various types of machine learning systems. For instance, when you browse through Amazon, you are offering the internet a lot of information about you (even if you are doing it unconsciously).

If you are searching for cribs, the internet knows that you are either expecting a baby or someone close to you is. If you are searching for a particular book, the internet knows you are interested in a topic (e.g. you might be interested in improving your self-confidence, so the internet will know that you might have issues in that area).

On top of that, the information you are posting on social media, the ads you click on, the sites you go to - they all define you as a human. While you may not be shouting out loud every password you have and every single move you make on every single day, you are feeding plenty of data into these huge information centers.

GDPR (General Data Protection Regulation) came as a reply to all the issues that come with a huge amount of data feed. According to this European regulation, users have the option of *choosing* whether or not their data is used for certain purposes. You may opt in or opt out - but your specification has to be crystal clear, and you have to be provided with all the ups and downs of choosing one option or the other.

GDPR is one of the possible ways of dealing with personal information and how it is managed by various companies, with various purposes. Probably the most relevant example in this sense is the Facebook and Cambridge Analytica scandal of 2018. In the wake of the scandal, the people of America woke up to a reality they weren't fully conscious of until then: what they do online has real consequences in real-life, even if their actions are very much innocent. And the reason this happens is because there are companies maneuvering tremendous amounts of data - about you, what you do every day, the things you click on, and even the things you merely stop to watch while scrolling through your Facebook feed.

All in all, there are three main issues you should be looking at when offering or collecting data about yourself, respectively about other people:

- Transparency: what data is being collected and what data is being shared with third parties?

- Control: how is your data shared and used? For instance, you might be OK to share your data for medical research purposes, but you might not be OK with being re-targeted in ads after visiting a site.

- Time limits: how long can they use your data? Just because you are OK with sharing information about yourself now, it doesn't mean it will always be so.

The data issue must be looked at from the other side of the fence as well. If people are so scared to share information about themselves, how will marketers and AI programmers get the data they need to move on with their endeavors? As mentioned before, there is no AI without data to feed into it - but how do you convince people that sharing information about their medical history can save lives, and how do you convince people that sharing data about their book preferences might actually give them some pretty good reading suggestions for their next vacation?

Clearly, the Cambridge Analytica scandal has shed a new light on this entire matter, and it has done it for all the participants in the data, "game": users, data collection companies, marketers, companies, and so on.

How do you create balance without making people feel they are stolen their privacy, but still make advances in the field of artificial intelligence? Considering how outraged a lot of users were when they learned what Facebook was doing with their information, it can be fairly assumed that this might be a pretty significant bump in the road.

Deep Learning and Jobs

While some may be afraid, "foreigners" are stealing their jobs, others are fully conscious that there is a fiercer competitor coming from behind: one that has no skin color, speaks no human language, and has no cultural heritage to bring with it in the workforce.

Machines have been stealing people's jobs ever since the industrial revolution - and up until now, nobody can say that leaving certain tasks into the hands of robotics hasn't proved efficient in terms of economic growth and general productivity.

Few trades are left outside of the heavy robotization process, and this means a lot of people are losing their jobs. When the world doesn't need manual carpenters and seamstresses anymore, where do you go?

Arguably, manually-worked objects tend to be better valued on the market precisely because they go beyond the mechanization process. But even so, not every carpenter can be a home designer, just like not every seamstress might want to be an actual fashion designer either.

Even more, machines are slowly moving into the world of intellectual jobs as well. What happens when we won't need doctors, teachers, engineers anymore? When artificial intelligence will be able to smoothly heal, educate, and engineer their own systems?

What will *we*, humans, be left with?

There will be a small subset of jobs still available, particularly those related to programming machines and those related to somewhat monitoring their activity. But beyond that, we might be looking at a jobless future.

This is a very heavy debate to have, because there will always be people saying we've got a long way to run before we reach the point where the entire mankind will be left without jobs.

The idea of a Universal Basic Income comes to complement the ethical issues connected to leaving 90% of the world out of jobs. Basically, what this idea brings to the table is that everyone should be offered a certain amount of money with a specific periodicity if they cannot work.

This should not be perceived as, "free money", though, and building such a system can be truly troublesome, especially in the United States, where social security rarely covers you for anything in case of unemployment.

There are several questions connected to the Universal Basic Income (UBI):

- Where would states get that money from? Some suggest that companies that employ full automation should pay higher taxes to cover for the Universal Basic Income. But how is this fair to companies, how does it affect their decision to automate, and what are they left with once they sack all their employees to save money, only to spend more on taxes to pay the same people without receiving their time and skill in return?

- How do you calculate this income? Different people have different needs, and we could, of course, build a machine to make fair calculations on what everyone's basic needs consist of. But how, "basic" should the basic income be? Should it barely cover for the bare necessities, or should you be allowed to live a comfortable life? Should it give you the freedom to do what you want and move how you want?

- What happens with those who might spend this income on fueling substance addiction? Should they be punished somehow, or should they be left to spend their money as they want? In the end, nobody punishes you if you want to spend your entire monthly paycheck on drugs - so why would a Universal Basic Income limit your spending to only a specific group of expenses?

- Will UBI close the financial gap between men and women? Despite popular belief, studies show that most women make less money than men. Will the Universal Basic Income close the gap, or simply go on with it?

- From a feminist point of view, how will UBI affect women's implication in the workforce? Will their work at home be recognized in "points" that add to their income?

- What will people do? If people don't have to work anymore (because they have no other option), where will their energy go? Will they be more inclined to higher rates of criminality or not?

- Will the economy grow? And if yes, what is the maximum growth it will be able to achieve? If not, where will this all lead us?

- What happens if, one day, we lose our artificial intelligence? By that point, it will be generations and generations into the implementation of full automation, so most people would have lost the basic skills to do a wide range of jobs, including medicine, engineering, trade jobs, and so on.

- Will the Universal Basic Income reduce poverty? But will it reduce the number of people living well above the line as well? And if yes, is this ethical? A Robin Hood-esque approach that, "takes from the rich to give to the poor" sounds romantic, but do keep in mind entire political systems were built on this idea and failed dramatically (just Google utopian socialism, for example).

- Will people be healthier? Not having to deal with long hours of work, sitting or standing for all these hours, stress, poor eating habits, and so on might make people more likely to be healthier. But then again, with so much time on their hands, will they actually go out to run or simply sit in front of their TV sets all day long?

- Will people continue to socialize? We spend 8,9, or more hours a day with our workmates. Inevitably, this can fill a socialization gap in our lives. What happens when this is removed?

The list of questions can go on and on, endlessly, but the main idea behind it is that AI *can* lead to a world without jobs and that this *can* have a huge impact on your entire life.

Although an entirely automated future might seem very far away, it might be closer than you think. In fact, if you are a Millennial, you might actually live to see this happening.

This is precisely why it is extremely important for everyone to acknowledge the importance of having these discussions *now*, so that we can prepare for the future.

This might not be fully connected to your activity as a programmer, but as a participant in this industry, you should be familiar with the ethical issues it might bring along - including unemployment and the necessity to implement an automation-related Universal Basic Income.

Deep Learning and the End of the World (As We Know It)

You don't have to be a Science-Fiction aficionado to realize that AI is bound to change the world - in many respects, for the better, but in many other respects, for the worse.

Deep learning can change your health, the way you eat, where you live, and even how you earn your money.

The end of the world may not come by AI nuclear bombs - but the end of the world as I, you, and everyone else know it is closer than we would like to believe.

What is your role as a programmer in all of this?

Are you the enactor of a new, more productive, healthier, happier world?

Or are you the harbinger of bad news?

In the end, I believe this is the kind of *choice* only you have to make. If you participate in machine learning projects that go beyond what you are normally comfortable with from an ethical point of view, you should make a retreat.

If, however, you participate in something you genuinely believe in, something that inspires you to dream of a better world, then, by all means, stick with it.

This book's main goal was that of introducing you to the deep learning and Python: what they are, how they can be connected, and what your job and implications are as a developer.

We're not here to discuss philosophy or the negative implications of machine learning - but hopeful, this chapter has helped you "round up" the main ideas behind machine learning and create a bird's eye view, one that will help you take the right decision for yourself as a programmer and for the machines you are programming as well.

Conclusion

Without any trace of doubt, machine learning and deep learning are two of the most exciting and interesting fields of study at the moment.

There are, truly, a million reasons to love artificial intelligence in general:

1. It is mankind's offspring

2. It brings together multiple disciplines

3. It improves productivity and efficiency

4. It is torn out of a SF movie (and yes, this might actually be a reason for some)

There are a lot of reasons to fear the advent of the AI era as well - starting with the fact that it comes with serious ethical implications and ending with the fact that nobody can tell you just how far AI will go and how, "sentient" it will become.

The book at hand did not aim to be a manual in Python or programming or even deep learning in general - but an incursion into the *realm* of these subjects, a short trip to make you curious about what Python and deep learning are all about, why they are used in association, and even *how* they are used, at times.

I know you will take the information presented here and use it to the best of your abilities, helping yourself create the future you want for your children, nephews, or simply neighbors.

Because, yes, as a data programmer, you belong to the future just as much as robots do. This is great news, because it means that even if everything in the world will be automated, your skills might still be needed. And it's great news from the point of view of the job satisfaction you get as well - because who doesn't love being useful and creating something as awesome as machines that are capable to save lives, predict financial situations, or simply make entertainment...more entertaining?

My purpose with this entire book was to show you that although deep learning is a truly intricate subject and that there is *a lot* to it, you can still be part of it if you put your mind to it. Python programming is, as I have repeatedly said it throughout the book, one of the easiest types of programming you can learn.

Its intuitive nature and the fact that you don't have to know how to program in more, "elevated" languages make it a truly beginner-friendly programming language even for people who have not written a line of code in their entire lives.

So, if you are interested in the realm of deep learning and the fascinating innovations it brings to the table, if you want a job that is future-proof or if you simply want to take on a challenge you will always remember, Python is for you. Even more, Python for deep learning is for you too, even if you have zero experience in programming.

Hopefully, I managed to instill curiosity in you - by showing you how simple Python can be, by showing you what artificial intelligence is all about, and by showing you clear examples of how AI is used in everyday applications without you even knowing about it.

Maybe even more importantly, I hope I helped you understand that AI and deep learning are not evil (or at least not inherently so), and that there are important ethical issues we should all discuss before it's too late in any way.

There are, of course, many other things that could have been discussed, beginning with the actual intricacies of Python and ending with newly arising ethical issues. What I meant to do is cover the very basics: the things you should absolutely know when you start showing an interest in this amazing field of science.

Because, yes, deep learning is a science by this point. It may have been fiction at the beginning of the 20th century and it may have been seen as delusional towards the middle of the same century but today, in 2019, deep learning is as real as it gets.

Artificial intelligence is, without the slightest trace of doubt, the final frontier in man-made computational sciences. It is the ultimate goal - the one that might help us live longer and happier, the one that might help us find a solution to the fact that we cannot exceed the speed of light, the one to help mankind make decisions based not on emotions and hunches, but on raw data.

Sure, this comes with its downfalls, as it was discussed in the last chapter of this book.

But if you are ready to embrace it all, you are ready to face the future with the largest possible smile on your face.

If you are ready to embrace Python even as a complete beginner, you are a daring soul who deserves to be part of the amazing future we're building in this industry.

If you are ready to embrace deep learning not just as a mere user, but as a programmer lying behind the inner works of these neural networks, you are a true pioneer in the grand scheme of things.

Hopefully, my book here has instilled all these sentiments in you - and it has made you ask all the important questions too.

What's next?

Get down and dirty with Python, learn its basics, and start coding. Just like riding a bike, writing programs for machine learning cannot happen without those first awkward steps - so stay optimistic, erase, try again, erase again, and then try once more.

The future is at your fingertips.

Use it wisely!

References

PEP 20 -- The Zen of Python. (2019). Retrieved from https://www.python.org/dev/peps/pep-0020/

Stack Overflow Developer Survey 2018. (2019). Retrieved from https://insights.stackoverflow.com/survey/2018

www.ingramcontent.com/pod-product-compliance
Lightning Source LLC
Chambersburg PA
CBHW071203050326
40689CB00011B/2232